Super

William Gilbert wo   3,
travelling all over   ·s
and eventually superyachts, while simultaneously
pursuing a career as a professional writer.

OTHER WORKS BY WILLIAM GILBERT

Novels

Supertanker Port of Call Asia

Supertanker Port of Call Cartagena

Supertanker Port of Call San Francisco

The Captain's Daughter

Pink Taxi

Short Stories

London Transport, Tales of London Life

Supertanker Captain and other stories

Marie of Gizo and other stories of the Solomons

Travel and other writings

Supertanker Circumnavigation

Cuba Port of Call

SUPERTANKER MEMOIRS

BY

WILLIAM GILBERT

Book cover design by The Book Design House

Contents

Supertanker Memoirs

Initiation

I sat in an office in the Gorbals in Glasgow. The taxi driver had reacted with mock horror when I'd asked him to take me there. I'd understood little through his thick Glaswegian accent, apart from the fact that someone with my own, English, accent might not be safe and did I want to see where Jimmy Boyle was from. I'd just smiled, inanely, which was my habit when Scotsmen whom I couldn't understand started to speak to me in London pubs, smiling until they frowned and then giving them an understanding nod.

The taxi slid to a stop outside a building which didn't look particularly derelict or even run-down. Soon, I was in an office with a middle-aged Scotsman with a greying combover and an untrustworthy look on his face. I was having a last stab at getting into the merchant navy. There'd been a massive shake out just when I was leaving school. The old British companies were collapsing, containerisation was aiding progress by causing redundancies and inflated profits for City wheeler-dealers. The more British seafarers the shipping managers for the big oil companies could get rid of the more likely that the British government would reward them with a knighthood for services to British Industry. It was the eighties.

Alarmed by the realisation during the run up to the full-on sailing of the fleet to sort the Argentinians out, during the Falklands War, that all the redundant British seafarers hadn't been sitting at home waiting for a call to duty for the last twenty years, since they'd been fired, and that the Government now couldn't find enough British merchant seamen to run all the ships they'd chartered for the expedition, the authorities had hastily taken up the suggestion of a Scottish businessman to set up a Government-assisted training scheme. There was a sort of vetting, but as the agency was being paid more of an administration fee than anything else, the age limit had been raised slightly which meant a few slightly older candidates than normal could gain entry into the merchant navy through them. I was one of them.

I signed what I had to sign. I would be assigned to some company; I didn't have any say in which. This wasn't a charity or a dating agency. I was sent back to Glasgow train station for the long journey home. I can't remember if they paid for the ticket. I was in such a passion to achieve my life long dream that I wasn't asking any questions.

I was desperate to join this declining industry. The salaries were never going to be spectacular. The portion of the public that still remembered what the merchant navy was had little respect for sailors. The Government, although sort of coming on side, didn't either. The shipping offices which once signed on and processed papers for tens of thousands of British merchant seamen when the ships flying the Red Duster shifted goods and people all over the thirty per-cent of the world which was part of the British Empire were now little hovels with dusty guidelines which no staff had had cause to read for years. But there was little romance in Mrs Thatcher's Britain, apart from the highly unromantic, New Romantic musical movement. It was all about getting rich and I wasn't particularly motivated by financial incentives. I wanted travel and excitement. The Shipping Companies Institute still produced the odd recruitment brochure, which would have been rejected by the Advertising Standards Association if it'd been brought to their attention, depicting happy officer cadets sailing under the Golden Gate Bridge, still holding up sextants, obviously requiring verification of their vessel's position, and not what I was to find was the reality i.e. checking tanks in filthy, sweaty boiler suits, having had no off- duty period longer than six hours for more than a week. But I still believed in the dream.

I thought we'd all join ships straight away, but there was a month at the former School of Navigation at Warsash. This once august institute, had been undergoing a long period of colonisation. Independent institutes were not part of the vision of the modern educationalists, everything should be shepherded into Institutes of Higher Learning and eventually polytechnics which grandly rebranded themselves as universities. I got to this place while the brave fight was still going on and it was still, just barely, under the control of the sort of gimlet-eyed, bearded captains who'd seen ships across the Atlantic in convoys during the war. It was unusual in that everyone there, from the newest entrant to the principal was motivated by a passion. Whether it's still like that now that it's been subsumed into the grand communism or totalitarianism of the modern British education system, I don't know.

It was very rare that, even among the students, people talked about likely salaries or possessions. The guidelines from the Scottish agency had said that we could consider taking CD players to sea. Most of the students didn't have them and wondered if they should go out and buy them. Finally, it was decided that this was just a suggestion and not a requirement; most teenagers would have considered them to be essential. This was the last band of romantics in an unromantic world. Traditional industries, of which this was very much one, were finished and I.T. and the ripping-off of widows and orphans' funds in the City with inflated commissions was going to rule, but we either didn't know it or didn't care.

Training

Soon, I was on a jet to Houston. This was exciting. It was my first time on a long-haul plane and I enjoyed the experience even though I found that the stewardesses didn't smile as in the posters, and that the other passengers were quite rough in the undignified scramble to secure the few empty rows of seats for sleeping.

I soon realised that I wasn't the only member of the new crew for our tanker on board the plane. This was the dying days of the British Merchant Navy other ranks. They'd got rid of the old school, violent lot who were kept under control by even more violent chief mates, but the remains were still quite boisterous. The American stewardesses banned them from having any more drinks after just a few hours and I wasn't quite sure, but I think I heard 'F.B.I.', mentioned, threateningly, before they all slumped into their seats and started flicking through the airline magazine.

Upon arrival, we were lined up in a special immigration line. The steward, wearing a great coat that I considered would probably boil him to death once we left the air-conditioned terminal, tottered around, clutching an open bottle of whiskey. In these days of Homeland Security, he would, I think, have been carted off to jail, but this was when the local men on the spot still had some semblance of autonomy and the chief immigration officer just wanted them all out of his terminal and away into the city where they would only hang around for a few days before they shipped out on some tanker. The big oil companies had a lot of clout and they wouldn't want any hold-ups with ships at their terminals.

We were soon stamped in and bundled into a mini van and taken to an American budget-chain hotel. We were going to spend two days in this hospitality desert.

Another trainee and I trailed round behind the British A.B.s, from gun shops to strip clubs. They seemed to know an alarming amount about firearms. I thought it best not to ask how. Some got quite jealous when a stripper lavished attention on me, which wasn't entirely unjustified as they'd been buying all the drinks and had given me a dollar to put in her G-string which was a mistake on their part.

Our two days of alleged bliss came to an end, alleged, that is, by the mate, who, every
time we asked to go ashore over the next six months would say, "You had two days in the hotel in Houston, that's more than I did, you ungrateful gits," ad nauseum.

The ship, itself was a wreck: streaked with rust, full of leaking valves. Nowadays, it would be slung out of the terminal before it was loaded, but this was over thirty years ago.

The captain was an imposing figure who exuded authority, something I was always to find difficult to do when I later became a captain, but it was easier for him. He was fair and honest and everything, but he wasn't soft-hearted or easily swayed by sob stories as I was.

The engineers were a gang of embittered Scots. The cook was the quintessential Liverpudlian. The bosun was a terrifying individual from the West Country who'd been known to knock out obstreperous seamen. Again, he wouldn't get away with that today. They'd be a court case etc.

The third mate was a bit of a Jekyll and Hyde. The second mate was a cheerful boozer. The mate was a total machine. He was nicknamed Roadrunner after the cartoon character. He never tired, never faded. He was super-efficient. He was also highly intelligent and, thus, bored out of his brain by a job which ninety-nine per-cent of the time consisted of staring out of a window. Of course, the other one per cent of the time was quite tricky: loading or unloading cargo. That occasional challenge wasn't enough to keep him entertained, though.

We loaded jet fuel into our huge cargo tanks at the terminal until our draught was at the limit for our berth and then we went on down the Houston ship canal and moored between a pair of buoys while we topped-off from barges. Subsequent to the surprise on the airline and at the hotel that American service staff did not uphold the spectacularly high service standards the world had been led to believe, I was a little shocked to find that America's safety standards weren't that high either. The bargees casually pumped jet fuel aboard while taking long drags on cigarettes, clad only in wifebeaters, tatty shorts and flip flops.

I endured three years of training on this company. I was kind of getting the impression that their employees were the sort who just couldn't cope with the disciplinary rigours on the likes of Shell and B.P., but they were giving up a lot in not working for them. There was no sort of company employee care on this company. The superintendents weren't bothered about welfare at all. And I wasn't a hundred per-cent certain that their safety procedures couldn't be improved. I was stood at the top of a tank being filled with jet fuel once, with the company's chief superintendent. There was a suspicion that a valve at the bottom of the tank was seized, and the mate and the second mate went down the ladders and wading through this highly-flammable liquid and then started wrenching valves. It turned out there was no problem with the valve, but I wondered what it would have cost to check it out without danger. The cargo so far loaded would have had to be sucked out either with the ship's own equipment or something supplied by the terminal and then then the tank washed and ventilated. A day's charter fee plus penalties? Thirty thousand dollars?

Another time, in Japan, some machinery in the engine room caught fire during loading. The engineers just cheerfully put it out with fire extinguishers and we didn't even inform the terminal or halt cargo.

I suppose, in some way, it made one proud to be British. There were all these foreigners with their fanatical safety routines and we just gaily carried on.

They moved me from the oil product tankers to gas tankers. These were supposed to be more dangerous, but no gas tanker had ever actually blown up; plenty of oil tankers had. I preferred the gas tankers because they were cleaner. They didn't stink. Cleaning the tanks was easy because of the smooth cylindrical design. It was still bizarre that you were allowed to go inside tanks which had been full of poisonous gases and clean them out, but that was the way. This procedure was beginning to become remotely controlled. The oil tankers normally had single-bottoms. This meant that the ships ribs were inside the tanks and these trapped dirt and debris. Once the environmentalists, who didn't really know enough to dictate ship construction policy, but knew enough to be difficult, had got to the governments, this type of construction was banned and ships had to have double bottoms, i.e. plating over the ribs. This made cleaning easier and sometimes physical entry into the tanks unnecessary.

I liked tankers in some ways, because I felt they were still ships. They looked like ships. Container ships didn't; they were just very large barges

Something which never seemed to change

was that our officers loathed the company. This was a surprise to me as most of the other companies' staff whom you came across loved their companies. The third officer, who'd been made redundant from P and O shortly after risking life and limb as a sixteen year old on the S.S. Uganda in San Carlos Sound, was always telling us company loyalty did not or should not exist anymore. The old system, in which boys went to sea with one company and died on their ships or for the lucky few made retirement forty-five years later, was gone. Still, an old captain at Warsash had said to us, after a quick look around to make sure no other staff were listening, "Boys, you are entering a declining industry. You are the last upholders of a proud British tradition." A few people had snickered, thinking he was just bitter and twisted. He hadn't been.

Suspicious Minds

Seamen were, traditionally, a notoriously suspicious lot. I was a sceptic about most things and actually laughing when I found myself on the receiving end of one crew's witchfinder-style persecution. I was up forward with the mate and some of the A.B.s while we were tying up. The mate had me relaying the orders from the bridge, trying to break me out of my shyness and build up my confidence, I think. The Captain said we had to come ahead a metre and the A.B.s started slipping the ropes, which was the correct thing to do if we were going to come ahead, and I said, "No, tighten them," and they told me in no uncertain terms to shut up. Suddenly, I'd known, somehow, that it'd turn out that we'd overshot and would need to come astern two metres to line our manifold up with the shore pipes. I think I had simply been doing a running sum in my head of all the little shifts we'd been doing, edging backwards and forwards to line up the manifold. Some information might have been misheard on the bridge and this might have caused confusion. "But we're going to need to come back two metres, anyway, "I blurted out, defensively. The A.B.s glared at me. If the mate hadn't been there, they might have thought of thumping me. Suddenly, the captain's voice came very loud over the radio; "Two metres astern." The A.B.s jaws fell. I could see they were torn between being angry with me, confusion and wonder: we were too far away from the middle of the ship to discern from looking at the manifold whether we had been in position or not. They tightened up the springs, drawing the ship back.

Later on, the mate looked at me strangely in the cargo office. The bosun had been up to see the captain. They didn't want someone with "other powers" on board. I found this out and was aghast. The captain passed me in the alleyway. "So, Willy," he said - he would never call me William - "you have strange powers." I thought he was joking.

"Well, my mother is part Romani," I said with a smile.

"So, you admit it," he said. I was dumbfounded.

Nothing came of all this. They couldn't very well send a telex and request that a trainee be taken off because he was a wizard. But the A.B.s were never the same with me. They always seemed to be deciding between hitting me and being frightened of me.

However, a few years later, my scepticism about the paranormal was blown away. I was third mate on a tanker which had had Korean junior officers before the company realised that they weren't any longer any cheaper than British officers, so they might as well switch back.

I'd just joined, and, due to some stupidity, the third officer was obliged to check the fire extinguishers in the engine-room, even though there were four engineers and three motormen down there at different times during the course of the day. I was just wandering along on one landing and I caught a glimpse of a bulky guy over the other side of the engine room in the electrical store. I turned to the fire extinguisher which I'd been examining, checked its plastic tag and the service date on the label, and looked up to wave at the other man. He'd disappeared. This was surprising. The electrical store was just a cage, through which I could see, and the ladder down to the deck was very long; he couldn't have walked down that in the time.

That evening, I was sitting in the bar after midnight with the fourth engineer. "Sorry I didn't wave to you this afternoon," I said. He looked up at me from the other side of the bar.

"What?" he said.

"When you were in the electrical store. It had to have been you. It was your watch and the Filipinos are too skinny. He looked angry and I wondered if I'd offended him with the implication that he was fat, though he seemed to be taking far more offence than that should have given. He swore at me, and I recoiled.

"What?" I said, with my arms spread out.

"Someone put you up to this," he said, "or you know."

"Know what?" I asked him. He seemed to be considering whether to risk falling into a trap.

"The last Korean electrician gambled away five months earnings and hung himself in the electrical store," he said.

"I didn't know," I protested. "Anyway," I said, hurriedly, "it was more of a shadow." The fourth engineer seemed to decide that I wasn't having him on.

"People have seen things," he said. I shrugged. Just then a tapping started. It was a metallic sound and appeared to be right between us. I looked at his hands, both flat on the bar. My hands were flat on the bar, too. I looked down. There was nothing metal to kick on my side of the bar. I looked up at him He was white. "Is that you?" he said. I shook my head.

Eventually, the tapping stopped. We decided to lighten the mood by putting porn on the T.V.

On the way to breakfast in the morning, I passed the second engineer. He was a tough Scot, and therefore, I thought, unlikely to believe in superstitions. "So, you've seen the ghost," he said to me.

"So, it's true?" I asked him.

"Speak to Miguel," he said. Miguel was one of the Filipino motormen. Later that afternoon, I found him.

"So, you've seen something?" I asked him.

His eyes turned bright and he seized the lapels of my boiler suit.

"You have seen it, too?" he said. "The shadow?"

Geordieland

I had an interview with a Geordie company. Any mention of this company always raised a smile. Gossip surrounded them. "Scrap ships run by Geordie engineers for the benefit of Geordie engineers; hotbed of Freemasonry. Don't go as third mate, you'll be running up and down the engine-room stairs all day long with your medicine kit." "Do they have a poor safety record?" I asked, naively, upon hearing the last. "No, they knock seven bells out of each other," came the reply."

I took the train to Geordieland and found myself sitting in a large office opposite a man who looked pretty tough. Up there, getting girls is still a matter of looking like the guy who can chase down the antelope and skin it most efficiently. This guy looked like he would have had plenty of girls in his time.

He ran through the usual tissue of lies. "Our ships are old but good." Oh yeah? I wondered why they suddenly had a vacancy. They were a very close-knit company, almost a family. They didn't like taking in outsiders, certainly not Southerners. Anyway, I got the impression it was fairly urgent. It turned out to be not as urgent as all that, though.

"You'll have to take a drugs test," he said. "His tone of voice made it sound as though he were making a veiled accusation, but I was to find out he always sounded like that. "Only we had a young guy go mental and we had to send him home," he said. "Killed himself, eventually. Cost the company a lot of money." I must have looked horrified, because he seemed puzzled by my expression and then added, too hastily, "Of course, it was very sad, too." He continued to stare at me. "Drugs were to blame," he said. I later found out from other officers that'd been on board during the incident that drugs were in no way to blame, but companies don't like it put down that their staff just "went mental". Much better to have some outside agent to blame. I was wondering whether I should just get up and walk out, but decided against it.

The boss's assistant saw me outside his office in, what I suppose was, the operations room. "We'll sort you out with this drugs test and then send you out," he said. I was a little bit offended by the drugs test idea. Of course, these days, it's probably mandatory. Why didn't the managers have to take them. They might come in to the office drugged-up and send out a demand that the captain do something stupid. Actually, shipping company managers are demanding that captains do stupid things, but under the influence of commercial pressures, not narcotics, and they're always careful to make sure that, officially, the final decision is the captain's and that their bullying and threats are just suggestions.

I passed the drugs test, which was easy as I didn't do drugs, having been in just about the last year to pass thorough the comprehensive school system without being exposed to them. I was at school when smoking was still the great evil. I didn't do that either, actually, but never mind.

Disappearing Ships

Actually, the first ship this company sent me to turned out not to be a tanker, but a bulk carrier. At this time, bulk carriers were sinking all the time. They'd mainly been built during a boom twenty years before and the combination of thinning, rusted steel and the increased speed with which terminals were loading them had caused them to succumb to stress. Mainly, they just disappeared. One captain told me that eight ships had disappeared after leaving Dampier alone and if the super-keen safety bods in Australia were carrying on like this without bothering to reduce the risks there wasn't much hope any other nation would. The newer ships were being built with high-tensile steel which wasn't much better than thinned-out, conventional steel. And, apparently, they were built to cope with an eight-metre wave. One captain with whom I sailed asked a Korean yard manager on a sea trial what he was supposed to do if he hit a nine-metre wave. "Well, you're on your own," the manager had replied. There'd been a documentary about all this on T.V., with Tom Mangold. Unusually for a media report on shipping, it had actually got everything right. It had little effect, though. Why should it?

Just to add to my apprehensions, I was joining this boat in Canada, to go on the top route to Japan. The idea behind this route was that some office bods thought that the tops of the highs would push you along. This company had already almost lost one ship doing that. The side plating had come away from the frames. The technical superintendent in the U.K. had suggested that the captain was overreacting in demanding to go to a port of refuge once he'd limped across and perhaps the deck fitter could weld them back on. Sounds mad, but the technical superintendents are put under intolerable pressure from commercial forces, too.

They'd actually been a long court case in the U.K. over this sort of thing. A captain had ignored the charter's instructions and gone on the southern route. The shipping company lost the court case; the charterers won. Well then, you'd assume that the captain shouldn't be blamed if something went wrong. Well, yes, apparently, according to the judge, he's still to blame for the decision even if he didn't make it, because he's the captain. It's probably contempt of court to say what I and any other rational person would think about this judgement, but I think it's obvious.

Anyway, I was hauled out of the line at Vancouver for an immigration check. Why me? I wondered. I found out later that the immigration officers didn't want to bother speaking through interpreters to the Chinese and were reasonably sure that I, being a British seaman, would have everything in order and so they could get their quota of interviews up with minimal hassle.

Then I was on a plane to Prince Rupert Island. This was a fantastic place, though I didn't initially get to see much of it. There was a strike on and our ship was way out at anchor. We were put in a hotel for a few nights and then taken out on a launch. The Canadian boat drivers were full of themselves and going on and on about how brilliant they were. "Yeah, yeah," we said.

The strike finally ended, to the captain's outrage. He'd already spent two months out of his five months' trip blissfully sitting at anchor and had been hoping to spend the remaining three months doing the same. The official for the grain terminal whom the launch brought out got it in the neck. "This is not on," said the captain. "I was told the workers were intransigent." He'd been a trainee journalist for a few months before he resigned in a huff and went to sea and used a lot of long words.

"Grain is an essential service," said the official. "The Government can just order them back to work." The captain's face turned even redder.

"That'd never happen in Britain," he said. "The workers would just tell the Government to get stuffed. So much for 'The Land of the Free'."

"That's the United States," said the official, patiently.

The workers ignored the captain's exhortations to continue with their strike, and the ship was manoeuvred through the channel and onto the berth. This wasn't a total disappointment to the officers and crew as, like a lot of personally tough captains, this guy was frightened of the company and hadn't hired any launches to take the crew in for a jolly. They'd only been two runs-in in the ship's suffocating, enclosed lifeboat which had taken an hour a half to make the journey from ship to shore.,

The radio officer tried to get the ship's miniscule entertainment fund from the captain so that he could go and buy some books. The captain refused to turn it over. The next day, we found out why. He proudly announced that he'd hired a stripper with it who would be coming to put on a performance after lunch in the officer's mess. Reluctantly, he agreed that the Filipino crew could join the British officers on this special occasion.

I was a little bit offended when she turned up because she brought a minder with her, the implication being that we were all potential rapists. But anyway. Actually, I found the whole experience a bit weird. It's one thing looking at strippers in a darkened strip club, it's quite another to look at them in a messroom with bright sunlight pouring through the portholes. I'd never seen the point in strippers, anyway. Why pay women to tease you?

There were millions who were happy to string you along for free.

We soon got the grain loaded. I suppose the workers had had their pay stopped while they were on strike and were keen to make it up.

There was a revelation when one of the stevedores started proudly boasting about how he'd beaten up with impunity some native-American the previous night who'd got too lucky with some woman whom he fancied, himself. I'd thought Canada was some social paradise where everyone lived in perfect harmony. I didn't realise they, too, had an Indian population living in third-world conditions. They keep that quiet.

Once we were loaded, we set off on our dangerous passage for Saudi Arabia. This cargo was destined for Iran, but as there were international sanctions on Iran, we were to dump it on the quay in Saudi and it would then be sucked up and dumped into another bulk carrier which would take it to Iran. The Canadians could adopt an innocent look if the Americans started to berate them for dealing with their arch-enemies. "Who could have known?" This wasn't the only sanctions busting ship I was on. I took a few gas cargos out of Libya, too. Sanctions are for hurting little people in the hope they'll mount revolutions, not for hurting multi-nationals.

The captain was a depressive, which is often a little difficult for the third mate, in this case, me, as the third mate is a bit of a captive audience. You're up there from eight to twelve in the morning and eight to twelve in the evening. It's difficult for the third mate to say to the captain, "Go away, you're bringing me down with your tales of woe." This captain was one of a breed which you find a lot on deep-sea merchant ships: those who've missed out on their imaginary, one true love. Normally, this is some schoolgirl, half-remembered from their days in the fifth form whom they could have dated "if they'd only had the guts to speak to her". Once I sailed with a captain whose one true love whom he'd missed out on was a stripper in South East London who'd let him walk her to the bus stop after a lunchtime session in the local pub in which she'd been prancing around in a G-string. Even more tenuous relationships get built up in men's minds when they have month after month to brood. I used to feel sorry for the women some of these men had actually married, to be honest. Little did they know that their husbands spent some entire days wishing that they'd married someone else and letting everyone know about it.

"You're sad," said one of these guys to me on the bridge once.

"Oh yeah? Why?" I'd asked.

"You've never known love," he said.

"I've never been divorced and taken to the cleaners, either," I replied.

"You're so selfish," he'd said. "You have such a selfish view of love." Hah! I thought. It was entirely in a normal day's run after leaving port for someone to come up to me and start moping over a just-received Dear John letter. I would listen sympathetically, careful not to offer any advice as the psychological principle of transference would come into play and I would be shouted at, and I would think, well, probably she finally realised that you didn't really love her but were obsessed with someone else. This might have been unfair in a lot of cases. Often, the woman had simply realised that she could have the house, the car, the children and financial support without this bewildered, alien visitor turning up from this floating, minimum-security prison once or twice a year and disturbing her routine.

Saudi Arabia was alarming. It was quite a surprise to find, upon arrival, that no Saudi Arabian, apart from the King, seemed to have a job. Well, this is a little bit of an exaggeration, I admit. The ship's agent, who turned up in glorious flowing robes looking like Lawrence of Arabia, clearly had a job. Everyone else we saw was Western or Sri Lankan.

The Sri Lankan head stevedore used to sit in the cargo room with me in the evenings, regaling me with the stories of the week's atrocities in chop square: beheadings, amputations (if you can call severing a hand with a cleaver an amputation). He told me of a special punishment for possessing porn of which I'd never heard: peeling off the fingernails and pouring acid on the nail beds. That had to be an exaggeration or completely made-up. I expressed disbelief, but he insisted it was true. Then he offered to sort me or anyone else on board out with a Sri Lankan nurse. "Eh, no thanks," I said. I wasn't totally confident that the British Foreign Office would do anything for me were I to be apprehended subsequent to such a liaison. Apparently, imprisoned, Western tanker officers who'd accidentally polluted Saudi Arabia's pristine waters were lucky if their embassies sent them the odd food parcel; they certainly weren't defended; too many armaments were sold to Saudi Arabia.

Once the Sri Lankans had unloaded us and were cheerfully loading this sanctions-busting cargo onto the adjacent Iranian ship, we were free to go. "Where to?" I excitedly asked the capitano.

"Brazil," he replied.

"Yee hah," I said.

"Don't get too excited," he told me. "Not Santos."

"Must be a few brothels and bars," I said. "Not that I patronise brothels myself, of course. I'm thinking of the Filipinos."

"Of course," said the captain.

It was a long voyage down to Brazil, through Suez and the Mediterranean and then across the Atlantic. Suez was the usual mixture of interesting and infuriating. The Egyptian government refuses to just formalise payment, so all sorts of fees have to be paid in Marlboro. Actually, it is kind of semi-formalised in that the fees are standard amounts of Marlboro, but why don't they just use currency. It'd be a lot more transparent and easier to monitor.

Companies, who all have anti-bribery clauses in their "manifestoes", tell the captains it's a small price to pay to keep the ships moving. "Why don't they give it out to the crew then?" asked one Egyptian-official-hating captain with whom I was once talking (actually, that's perhaps a redundancy: all captains are Egyptian-official-hating). The companies don't, of course. Most of them actually make a company profit on the beer and cigarettes which they sell to their own crews. some even forcing the captains to impose a company tax if he funds the bond himself.

The journey was surprisingly peaceful. Even the South Atlantic was calm. We arrived at anchor off this little Brazilian coal port and sought to find out when we were berthing. We were told we had a while to wait, and then, a few mornings later, I was listening to the port radio when they called up another bulk carrier anchored in the bay. "We are ready for you," said the port.

"Captain very drunk," said the Filipino officer on watch. "Much vodka yesterday." There was a moment's silence. Then the port officer spoke again.

"May we speak to the chief officer," he said.

"Chief officer also very drunk," said the Filipino. There was a longer silence and then the port officer called up another ship.

"You can come in if you've fixed your steering," said the port officer.

"O.K.," said the watchkeeper.

"So, you confirm you've fixed your steering?" said the port officer.

"Steering working good," said the watchkeeper, and then he added, thoughtfully, "sometimes." You could almost hear the port officer sighing over the radio. Then he called us up.

"Can you come in?" he said. "I called down to the captain.

"Yeah, sure," he said. He would be getting off when we got to Europe and was keen to get there ASAP. He eventually came up to the bridge.

"They want us to open our hatches prior to

arrival," I said to him.

"They can get stuffed," he replied. "That's against regulations." We did this all the time for cleaning. He was just being difficult. He wasn't about to be told what to do by a bunch of Brazilians.

We went onto the berth. Amusingly, a ship had snapped in half on this berth a while previously and the port officials had been surprised to find all the officers and crew in their Sunday best with their suitcases on the deck at the highest point on one of the two pieces into which the ship had split. This was a brand-new ship, albeit built with thin high-tensile steel, and while it would have been quite possible for it to fail during a sea passage, its splitting apart during its first ever loading seemed to signify an insurance job. Just in case, the Brazilians slung the captain and chief officer in jail. Actually, it would never have happened in Europe. The ship's loading plan had indicated completely loading the holds at each end of the ship first. The Brazilians had merely raised an eyebrow at this. In Holland or somewhere like that, the port would never have accepted such a plan. I can't say it wouldn't have happened in the United States, though. We were once there in one of the more backward states and the port tried to insist we used a loading plan of their own design which called for exactly this. There was a furious argument while the chief officer insisted the port used our own plan. We won, but there were plenty of "Sons of bitches," and "Limey m*****f*****s," before this conclusion to hostilities.

Once we were alongside, we found that the captain had been keeping a secret. He was going home earlier than had been thought. He was superstitious character and hadn't wanted to say anything in case he jinxed it, but we'd been wondering why he suddenly looked so joyful. This captain was a bit of a thug. The new captain, who turned up wearing a Panama hat and a blazer, was a gentleman. Captains seemed to divide pretty evenly between thugs and gentlemen, rarely anything in between. These were perhaps the only forms successful captains could take. The thugs carried the day by enforcing discipline; the gentleman, by bringing out the best in people. Companies tended to alternate on any particular boat between appointing one or the other. Thus, the thugs would bring order, but intimidate everyone. The gentlemen would turn up and restore sunshine but let things get a little lapse during their five or six-month trip, and then the cycle would begin again. I wasn't tough enough to become a thug. I thought I'd better work on becoming a gentleman.

On this company, the mates divided the day into eight-hour shifts in port. I volunteered for the four p.m. to midnight shift. Everyone thought I was mad, but this was what suited me. I liked to bimble around on my own in the daytime and see something. Though, this time, I took a taxi to the beach and nearly got my throat cut when I disputed the bill, which was about eight times what it should have been, so it wasn't always the best option. The rest of them liked to take a taxi in the evening to the nearest whore bar and stay there all night with the odd trip outside the establishment to the nearest hot-sheet hotel, in the company of a prostitute. "What's the point in journeying around?" I asked once. Couldn't you stay at home in Newcastle or Liverpool and do that?" Having been informed that I was a soft Southerner, I was asked to explain why I found looking at old churches so fascinating. "I didn't go to look at an old church," I protested. "I went to the city and then went to a beach." "And," said someone, "you would have got your throat cut if the mate hadn't come to the gate and saved you." He had a point there. "You shouldn't be going around on your own," he continued. Well, he was possibly right, but I endured their company and entire conversations about Newcastle generally and Newcastle football club in particular, night after night. Sometimes, even though their repartee could be delightful on occasion, I needed a break. "I don't have a map of Newcastle city centre imprinted on my brain and I don't care whether Newcastle football team wins or loses," I had said to them once. The latter was sacrilege. I think if the captain hadn't been a Yorkshireman, who seemed amused by this statement, I might have received a written warning.

Full with coal, we were soon on our way, up to Antwerp. We were quite happy about being full with coal and not iron ore. Iron ore is much heavier and thus when the ship is down to her marks, there are only little piles in each of the hatches which means if something breaks off such as a hatch cover or a coaming or the vessel is holed, there is more space which can be filled with seawater, causing the ship to sink. In addition to this, some either stupid or ruthless shipping company executives had decided that with iron-ore cargos, as the ship's maximum deadweight in iron ore took up so little room, holds could be alternately filled with cargo or empty, and the ship could be loaded more quickly, and thus port dues could be reduced. The fact that this increased the strains on the vessel, possibly leading to a lot of the unexplained sinkings which had been happening, was not considered.

Anyway, the Atlantic crossing went smoothly, but then we hit Biscay. Biscay is a bit of a git really. Just when you think you're home, safe and sound, you can get hit by terrible weather. This happened to us. We were forced to heave-to while the wind and the seas ripped deck fittings off. An eighty-foot accommodation ladder broke away and was clattering all over the deck. If it snapped off a hatch coaming, we'd have serious problems. The vessel might just split in half anyway, but assuming it didn't, we wanted to maximise our chances of survival. The chief officer, whom the previous captain had hated and never once stopped slaggingoff in conjunction with the second mate, bravely trooped out there with the Filipinos and lashed it down. Some of them could easily have been killed. This same company had actually had a mate swept off the deck in similar circumstances. All his fellow officers, looking on from the security of the bridge, had been cheering, as this mate was particularly hated. By a miracle, to their disappointment, another wave had swept him up and dumped him back on deck, and he'd managed to cling on and then make his way into the accommodation.

I was quite surprised by this captain's behaviour. We'd all thought he was really lazy and uninterested in anything, but, in this, he was an inspiration. He stood, legs apart, hands clasped behind his back, without a flicker of fear passing over his face. His white moustache didn't even twitch once.

Finally, I overheard him seek advice from the chief officer, or at least seek his opinion. This rarely happens, especially with experienced captains such as this one. "What do you think?" he said.

"Run for it," replied the chief officer. We did so. Well, we limped for it. We were soon out of it: the weather died down and we were sailing away from it.

We all thought our crisis was over. Well it was, but there was soon a new crisis. The chief officer hit a small coaster during the night. The collision made only a slight ding in our ship, but the coaster, due to the laws of momentum, suffered more damage. It didn't sink, though, and we weren't required to offer assistance. I didn't even find out about this until the morning when I went up on the bridge and found the chief officer complaining bitterly that it was unfair to blame him. They hadn't sounded the general alarm, and when one hundred and fifty thousand tonnes hits five thousand, the vessel weighing one hundred and fifty thousand tonnes doesn't suffer much of a shock.

We went into Antwerp, a port which all and sundry hated. The Belgians were uncooperative and spiteful at all times. Twenty-five per cent of the pilots on the river Scheldt were Belgians (the other seventy-five per cent being Dutch) and it was always difficult when you got one of them on board. Basically, though I believe this is not an original observation, they were Frenchmen without the Frenchmen's good points.

The thug-like manager who'd been bemoaning the cost involved in the run up to the boy's suicide, came on board to deal with the aftermath of the collision. I came on cargo watch just after he'd boarded, and he came down and ranted at me over the gangway net not being out. This is an easy one for government agencies to pick up on, so there is a lot of attention paid to it. I thought of mentioning that I'd just come on watch and the second mate had been responsible for rigging it up with the Filipinos, but I knew this manager didn't like me anyway, so splitting on the second mate wouldn't have done me any good.

The chief officer was sent home, still complaining that it was unfair to blame him. Under any other circumstances, he would have been delighted to be sent home early, and, so far, no one had actually blamed him. Shipping companies are very careful about that. Blaming and firing your own man after a collision is tantamount to admitting fault. Their own lawyers will tell them in no uncertain terms that they're idiots if they find out that they've done this.

I was going home, too, but other than that the manager hated me, I shouldn't have any justification for worry. I'd been scheduled to go home and I wasn't on duty when the accident happened. I did wonder, though. Did everyone onboard suffer a little in such situations? Guilt by association?

My name was still with a few recruitment agencies and I kept my c.v. updated with them as a matter of habit. With an utter cheek, the shipping company which owned the freighter our ship had hit rang me up with a spurious story about a possible vacancy and then tried to get me chatting about the accident. I politely said that I hadn't been on watch at the time and so didn't have any information. You never knew. I might need them sometime if I were fired. No point in being impolite. I thought about alerting my company to this, but then thought that it wouldn't do me any good. If I did, a rumour would soon develop that I was collaborating with the enemy. Best just to sit tight and wait until the company gave me a new appointment. It soon came.

This trip began with another Brazil departure, this time on a longer voyage: Japan via the Cape of Good Hope. One of the company's other ships had performed a similar trip, but the distance via either Cape being more or less the same, the captain had decided to go via Cape Horn for a change. In these halcyon days before real-time monitoring of ships' progress, the ship had emerged into the Southern Pacific before the company had realised what the captain was up to. The ship hadn't actually been insured to go that route, something of which the captain was blissfully unaware. Never mind. It didn't sink.

 This was a tedious journey, enlivened only by the handsome fourth engineer's fling with the chief engineer's fifteen-year-old daughter. I suppose all and sundry were guilty of something in that none of us informed her father. Once the captain found out what had been going on, he seemed quite grateful that no one had brought it to his attention as his hand would have been forced. He might have suspected, but without someone officially splitting on the fourth engineer, he could, as the Americans say, retain deniability. There was also the factor that if someone had, in addition to an incident of underage sex, he might have had a case of murder on his hands.

 There was a difficult moment for me. The

fourth engineer had been having sex with three or more Brazilian prostitutes a night, without a condom. After a month, his glands swoll up and he came to me, who being the third mate had been given responsibility for the medical locker, despite my not having a ship captain's medical care certificate. Having perused the Ship Captain's medical guide on occasion and this being the height of the AIDS hysteria, I suggested to the radio officer who was an ex-member of the Royal Corps of Signals and, so he said, the S.A.S. and thus believed to be tough and of good judgement, that the fourth engineer might be showing symptoms of H.I.V. infection. "Keep this to yourself," he said. "Just give him an aspirin and send him on his way." A month after the girl went home, she apparently experienced full-on glandular fever.

We arrived a couple of hundred miles off Japan and, the loading berth not being ready for us, the company told us just to drift. This is yet another of those semi-orders from a shipping company office which places the captain in a bind. It is no defence in the event that someone runs into you while you're drifting to say, I had the engines off because I was drifting, so I wasn't able to take evasive action. Yet, it is impractical to keep them running. It isn't good for them and it would waste fuel anyway. Neither the company nor the chief engineer would tolerate it. Technically, the captain has supreme command, but chief engineers on big ships have a lot of say, and companies have a tendency to get rid of captains who are sticklers for the rules when it doesn't suit the companies.

Aside from anything else, we quickly ran out of all food apart from rice. The Filipinos solved the problem. Every evening, one of them would be lowered with his foot in the loop of a mooring rope, from the poop deck, high above the water. When he was dangling just above the surface, he would spot dorado fish swimming around in the arc of light from the spotlight up above and spear them with a javelin attached to a thin line. The other Filipinos would then haul the fish onto the deck and send them down to the freezer.

This went on night after night until the captain went down below on his fridges and freezers inspection, opened the door of the freezer in which the fish were being stored, and was promptly buried by a fish avalanche. Once he'd been extracted, he announced that he thought we had enough fish on board for the time being.

I quickly got sick of rice and fish, but the Filipinos were quite happy. Presumably the company was quite happy, too, with its reduced feeding bill. I did once sail on a company who decided that as part of its vaunted ethical policy, Filipinos on board its ships were banned from fishing, but it wasn't this company.

I was actually coming in for a hard time myself from all the married men on board. They resented the fact that I was single and was therefore quite happily sitting silently while they moaned on and on about their wives and kids. They were always trying to bait me into an argument. Once I made the mistake of saying that I was frightened of getting divorced. "That's a stupid reason not to get married," they said, more or less in unison. When I went up on the bridge that evening, I was subjected to a further tirade of abuse and ridicule from the second mate, during his handover.

It wasn't so stupid though. I'd sailed with one second mate, on a different company, who'd gone on and on about his loving wife for months. Then she came on board. It was sickening to see them walking round hand in hand. I thought at the time that the behaviour of the cadet and some the British deckhands was a little bit furtive, but had been blissfully ignorant of the reason. Months later, on a different ship, I was to meet that cadet again and find out why. Every time the second mate had gone out on deck on watch, the cadet and/or some of the deckhands had been nipping into his cabin for a quick tryst with his wife. This second mate even used to sacrifice his leaves, going away to work for a month or so on coasters, to bring more money in for the family. Added to the frequent visitations to the bridge of officers seeking the good listener i.e. me and clutching tear-stained Dear John letters from their wives, this led me to be quite cynical about marriage.

On this ship, the mate was quite a tough nut: Scottish, known to have filled-in a few stroppy deckhands and one or two officers. He was going on about how he'd straightened out his step-daughter's older boyfriend (she'd been sixteen; the boyfriend, nineteen.) "I told him I'd cut his balls off if he hurt her," he gleefully informed me.

"How were you thinking he would hurt her?" I asked him.

"Well," he said, "for example if they split up."

"What happened after you gave him this warning."

"Well, he disappeared from the scene," he said, triumphantly.

"So," I said, "in order to prevent your step-daughter being hurt by her relationship with her boyfriend breaking up, you broke it up." His face flushed.

"Don't you get put against the wall," he said, infuriated. "You think you're so clever."

"It's the Socratic technique," I protested. "People won't listen to an explanation of their own contradictions, so you lead them round in a circle until they contradict themselves." This did not placate him.

"Don't quote stuff at me," he said. I decided to be quiet.

This mate also liked to lecture me on my selfish, bachelor lifestyle. His wife later divorced him, the judge kindly giving her the house which he'd built himself with his bricklayer father prior to his marriage, and his step-daughter carrying on with whomever she liked without his assistance in evaluating her suitors. He, sensibly, went to work running a manning agency in the Philippines. Probably, he has some dutiful, subservient Filipina wife now, enraging feminists in his former, married-life circle of friends back home who hear of it, with his happiness.

A small-scale sinking

There was one more little disaster during our three weeks of drifting around while our date for going in seemed to recede faster than time went on.

Filipinos are mad on American sports i.e. baseball and basketball, an obvious legacy of their colonisation and then following their independence, military occupation. I, along with a lot of British men was a bit prejudiced against both, baseball resembling the infants' game rounders and basketball resembling the schoolgirls' game netball. Anyway, they wanted to play basketball. They'd found a basketball stuffed down the bottom of some locker and their fitters had fabricated something resembling a basketball ring and screwed it to a plate above the poop deck. On their off-time, they proceeded to bounce around in their singlets, slinging the ball at it. This was the only time they went out on deck not bound up with rags like The Mummy as they were normally desperate to avoid getting tans and then being thought of as agricultural labourers, in the streets when they got back home.

Inevitably, after half an hour, the ball just went flying over the side. I wondered why the captain or the company hadn't thought of this way of entertaining them themselves and just sent on board about a hundred basketballs. They couldn't be that expensive. Anyway, I suppose this would have violated some company policy and led to less hors d'oeuvres at the annual shareholders' meeting or less money in the kitty for company officials to attend 'motivating your employees' seminars.

The Filipinos decided to launch the old draught-survey boat, which had been steadily rotting away in its brackets for twenty years. It wasn't part of the life-saving equipment so hadn't been subject to outside inspections and, quite possibly, hadn't even been used in all that time, as terminals provided their own draught-surveying boats. With boundless optimism, they launched it. I stood on the upper deck, wondering if this was a good idea. I wasn't about to split on them, however. Then the second officer, who was the safety officer, came out to watch. I felt some of the responsibility to inform on them lifting off my shoulders. Finally, the mate, who had already had his afternoon tipple, came out and started humming the Hawaii Five-O theme as they uncoupled the boat from the crane hook and paddled furiously to catch up with the ball, which was drifting away almost as quickly as they could paddle. Finally, when they were a couple of hundred yards from the ship, they scooped it up, and then started shouting and paddling even more furiously. The boat was sinking. With an alacrity which they had never displayed during working hours, they scooped away. The mate was genuinely amused; the second officer looked a little bit worried. There'd definitely have to be a blame game if they drowned or were snapped up by sharks, and he would be the most convenient scapegoat.

With the boat more or less full with water, they scrambled for the crane hook. The three of them were left suspended from it while the boat sank beneath them. It was too much hassle to launch the rescue boat so we brought them on board, one at a time, using the foot in the loop of the mooring rope technique.

"Game over boys," said the mate, once they were on the poop deck, shaking and dripping. "You should have been more careful."

The captain heard about the whole event later on, but, with his experience of the blame game, knew better than to send in any reports, and just raised an eyebrow. I don't know how the loss of the draught boat was ever explained. Perhaps none of the visiting superintendents ever noticed it was missing.

The Filipinos, shaken but not stirred, went back to their previous off-duty past time of singing 1970s' pop songs over the backing of their karaoke machine

Japan and Hyundailand

Once we'd left Japan, unhappy as the port at which we'd docked, Mitsushima, wasn't friendly and most of the bars had a no 'round-eyes' policy. "Maybe they still resent the atom bomb," said the fourth engineer. That was probably round here."

"Why was it probably round here?" I asked him, bemused.

"Well, Mitsushima, Hiroshima," he said.

"So," I said.

"Well, it's probably a local-style name," he replied.

"Shima just means island," I said.

"Yeah, well, it can't, clever-dick," he said. "Because Mistushima isn't even an island." I gave up.

"Anyway, you're not supposed to talk about the atom bomb," said the second mate.

"Why not?" asked the fourth engineer.

"It's embarrassing to the Americans," the second mate replied. "They like to be seen as the good guys. Plus it was kind of cheating and they like to be seen as the epitome of fair play."

"Epitome of fair play?" I said with a raised eyebrow.

"Yep," confirmed the second mate. This was the kind of endless, pointless conversation which got going when there weren't enough distractions. Luckily, there was soon a diversion. I discovered, by listening in on a conversation between the captain and the chief engineer, that we were going to the shipyard in Ulsan, Korea. I only found out ten minutes before the rest of them were told, but it was still satisfying to have information in advance of what I considered to be the hoi polloi.

Some of the older crew, which meant some of the engineers, were excited about Ulsan. 'Hyundai Town' they called it. "Miles of car factories," they said.

"So?" I replied.

"Eighty girly bars," they added. "Off limits to white women and Korean men."

"Sounds good," I said.

"The father at the mission got the push for allowing the hookers to hang out there," said the third engineer.

"That wasn't Ulsan," said the second engineer. This dispute soon escalated and someone had to jump in to separate them.

The information about the car factories and the 'pubic triangle' was definitely spot on, though. No sooner had we docked and I'd been given the daytime off, the first day on which there was any time off at all, I took a taxi from the port to Ulsan city. We passed some factory gates. "Hyundai car factory," said the driver. About ten minutes later and five miles further on, we passed some more factory gates. "Hyundai car factory," said the driver.

"Two factories?" I said.

"Same factory," he replied.

The shipyards themselves were incredible. They were launching one full-size tanker or bulk carrier every ten days and working on another thirty-five ships which were just there for haul-outs and repairs. Rumour had it that the whole thing had started just a few years before with one ship which Hyundai had built on spec.

The founder of Hyundai, who'd walked barefoot from the North after the Korean war, had built the whole company up from nothing. Typically, now all the politicians and unimaginative bureaucrats who'd forgotten that they only had a functioning country thanks to him had turned on him and were doing him for corruption. Weren't so keen to do him for corruption when he was saving the country, were they.

The pubic triangle was a revelation, too. There were no sight-seeing female Scandinavian backpackers and the like wandering the streets in there; this place was strictly business.

I arrived in a disgruntled state. We'd climbed the road to the top of the hill above the shipyards and stood around waiting for a taxi. A taxi arrived and I told the driver to turn round and head for where I was sure the pubic triangle was. The Geordies insisted it was in the other direction. They were wrong and we ended up in some kind of combined trainer shop/whore bar in the middle of another little town. The Geordies started saying we should get a taxi and go where we should have gone in the first place. I said, "We're here now; let's just stay here." Then, in a combined movement, they started to make it plain that I was just a nuisance and being difficult. "If you hadn't insisted on going the wrong way, we'd already be where we should have been," I complained. They weren't listening.

We bundled into a taxi and went back up the hill and down the other side. At the entrance to the pubic triangle, I told them I wanted to go off on my own for a bit. I wandered around outside it and found the red-light district for the Koreans. The girls in the windows looked horrified when I, a "Western monkey", looked in at them, and then I heard what I swear must have been the sound of a dog being boiled alive, and scurried back to the pubic triangle.

I found the Geordies all paired off in Madame Sue's, the leading young lady emporium. Their partners were smiling blankly at them, clearly baffled by their accents and wondering what language they were speaking. I saw one glance round, as if wondering if there were anyone who could assist her with translation, and then roll her empty glass in front of her paramour, the third engineer. He immediately bought her another drink.

I slunk out and ended up in The Hole in the Wall, the only Western food place in the triangle. There was some old boy, probably a British superintendent handling one of the repair jobs, sitting in a corner, and two waitresses, the Mama San and a big, placid-looking Canadian. One of the waitresses was extremely pretty and she smiled at me and I smiled at her. The Canadian stomped up to me. "That's my girlfriend," he said. I looked at him.

"Listen," I said, "you new in this sort of establishment?"

"First time out of North America," he said. "Been here a month."

"You're lucky," I told him. "I'm not a violent man, but some of the guys who come in here will not have seen a woman for five months and if they think they've got a chance and you're in the way…. Added to that, they might think you're threatening them, which they won't like. Plus, it's her job to flirt with the customers." He wasn't listening. I thought that it would just be a matter of time before he had his nose flattened. However, it was I who was almost on the receiving end of irrational violence.

A tall, sinister-looking individual, whom I later found out was an Argentinian, came in and violently gripped the other waitress's arm while I was sat at the bar talking to her. I looked up at him.

"Don't get angry or I'll get angry," he said.

"We'll, we'll see what happens," I told him. I wished, for once, that the Geordies were with me. They'd have sorted him out. My bluff wasn't called, and. with a disgusted look, he pushed the girl's arm away from him and stormed out.

"Be careful of that guy," said the big Canadian. "He's violent." Thanks for the assistance, I wanted to say, sarcastically, but I said nothing.

Then the Mama San started saying that we should clear out and that she wanted to go home.

Ungrateful bitch, I thought.

The Canadian left with his "girlfriend", and

then the other waitress went out and then the old boy and then I.

I'd no sooner got a few yards down the road than I saw the Argentinian shaking the girl while the Canadian looked on. Oh well, Bilbo, I thought, interesting place to die in. I wandered down there and the Argentinian turned round, glared at me and pushed the girl away. She scurried off. "I want to talk to you," he said.

"Oh yeah?" I said.

"Listen, we're all friends," said the Canadian. We manifestly weren't.

"I'm not talking to you; I'm talking to him," said the Argentinian. He turned to me and held out his hand.

"You are a very brave man," he said. "I am sorry." I shook his hand, trying to hide my delight. I'd been a hero, so far as I was concerned, and I hadn't been beaten-up. I smiled and said my goodbyes.

I found the Geordies, still in Sue's. I related my tale, breathless with excitement. To my disappointment, they were either outraged or disgusted.

"You don't take risks for these women," they said. "you just pay them and have sex with them. You could have been killed." So, I went from hero to being a stupid fool in my own mind, within moments.

Yet, there was an upside. For the rest of our month-long stay, as soon as I walked in the door of any establishment in the pubic triangle, the girls were all over me while paying the Geordies little attention. "You good man," they said. I tried to enjoy my fifteen minutes of fame, but I was shooting nervous glances at the Geordies. If they were to get jealous, it wouldn't be good for me.

Dealing with the Filipino mafia

There was another nasty incident for me on another ship, a tanker. We were in Antwerp with the loathsome Belgians. The Filipinos has been up the road with the second mate and gone to a Filipino club. This had been in the days before cheap mobiles, and generally the Filipinos used the public phones in the seamen's missions to ring home, once in a while, and find out if the new born was doing O.K. This time, they were lured into using the club's phones. The Filipina hostesses, invited them to do so, telling them that the bill would only be "small". Once the phone had done the rounds on the table and everyone was satisfied wife, brother, brother's wife ad infinitum were O.K. back home, the bills were presented. They were astronomical. Once the bouncers and owner had all gone into another room at the same time, our Filipinos gave them the slip, brushing the girls' grasping hands away and running down the road and jumping into taxis.

They made it safely on board and breathed sighs of relief. Phone bills of the equivalent of two hundred and fifty U.S. dollars or so were a lot of money for people who earnt in some cases, such as the steward's, as little as twice that a month.

The next day, someone from the crew rushed up to me while I was on cargo watch. "There is problem in galley," he said, breathlessly. Problem in galley, I thought. What's that got to do with me. I strolled off the deck to deal with it. In the United States, abandoning the deck like that while cargo was going on without the watchman being there, who was actually having breakfast, would have been an offence, but never mind; we weren't in the United States. In the crew mess, I found two scar-faced, obvious gangster Filipinos choking and shouting at the cook. I took the scene in and then told them to get out. The most evil-looking of them turned round and spat at me. Then they explained that the cook owed them money for the phone call. "So what?" I said. "Get off the boat." They ignored me. I was anxious for the captain not to find out about this until I'd got rid of them. I knew he'd make the cook pay. We had a gentleman captain on board and this time we very definitely needed a thug.

I went and found my watchman. He was a bulky guy who rarely smiled. His name was Osmando. I'd once been chatting to him with the second engineer, and the second engineer, who was familiar with the Philippines, had asked him what he did at home on his leaves. "I hunt communists," he'd said.

"And do you bring them back alive?" the second engineer had asked, jokingly.

"Sometimes," Osmando had answered. "If the police want to torture them for information." He was a very serious dude.

I walked into the galley again and told the gangsters, once more, to get out. They spat in my direction. Then Osmando walked in. Their faces changed. Something in Osmando's own face told them, I think, what their fate would be if they didn't get out.

The one who'd been choking the cook, threw him against the bulkhead and then they both walked out, cursing in Tagalog.

"What did they say?" I asked Osmando, who, inexplicably, looked worried.

"They say they come back with the police," he said. I scoffed at this.

"The police won't support them," I told him. How wrong I was.

The Filipinos sent some tearful Filipina girl on board the next morning, accompanied by a portly, red-bearded Belgian policeman. The second engineer glared at them. "What's going on?" he said to me.

"They've come over the Filipino cook's unpaid rip-off bill," I replied. "I think the others paid up."

"Captain should sling them off the ship," said the second engineer. "It's British territory." Actually, it was Hong Kong territory, which, I suppose, was more or less British territory in those pre-handover days. It's always been a bit of a grey area though, this the ship being part of the territory of whichever country in which it is registered. The authorities tend to make their decision on this issue in line with whatever view suits them at the time.

I rushed into the accommodation and saw Osmando trailing the Filipina girl up the stairs with his fist wrapped in bandages. "What did you do wrap your hand up for?" I asked him.

"Does not leave marks on skin?" he said. "You know, when you hit people." This seemed quite sensible.

"But," I said. "there's only a girl and the policeman. I don't think you can hit the policeman and you don't want to hit the girl." Osmando looked disappointed.

I went upstairs and the two visitors were sitting in the captain's salon. He looked up at me while the girl quietly sobbed. "They are blaming this poor girl," he said. "And they've forced her to make a complaint. Tell the cook I'll lend him the money to pay it." I sighed. There was no fighting this. The gangsters had outsmarted us; the Belgian police had supported them against decent hard-working sailors; the captain, a sentimental old fool, had been moved by the girl's crocodile tears. I went to find the poor old cook.

"Filipinos are always so nasty to other Filipinos," said the junior engineer, as I passed him. "That's what holds them back." I looked at him wondering what to say. "And the Catholic church, that, too," he added.

We'd all had enough of Belgium. We were

glad to leave. Shame we hadn't gone to Holland. I was to find that kind of schizophrenia in other geographical locations. When I was sailing in the Adriatic, I'd noted that in Croatia, the officials were all aggressive, the bureaucracy was a nightmare. Yet, sail out to sea, round the headland and into Montenegro and you were in a land of smiles and tranquillity.

Manilla's floating discotheque

We were at anchor off Manilla one time and the Filipinos came to us officers and asked if we wanted a party. The captain raised an eyebrow. "Two hundred dollars," said the Filipinos.

"What?" said the captain. "What sort of party?" The Filipinos shrugged.

"Party," they said in unison. "Disco. Lights, Some girls." The captain shrugged. We were in ballast. This wasn't a risk. This was still before Dick Cheney ruined seafaring with his homeland security scam which entailed all the ship's security gumpf, which, in a marvellous display of judicial overreach, the United States had managed to enforce over the entire world. This captain was a gent, not a thug, but this was no guide as to how he'd react to such a request: gents could be sticklers for proprieties and so could thugs. He gave permission. The Filipinos whooped.

The chief officer turned to me. "Don't fall in love, Willy," he said, "I know what a sentimental fool, you are?"

"They're just bringing hookers on board, anyway," I said.

"Won't deter you, I'm sure," he replied. "Anyway, you never know; they're on their home ground here; they'll be wheeling out their most beautiful cousins and maybe even little sisters. You're a catch. So would we all be if some of us weren't married."

Fairy lights, brought out from God knows where were strung up on the poop deck. The crew scrubbed up. For the British officers, this was a major ordeal. Skin stained with lube-oil was viciously scrubbed; out of control nasal hair was trimmed for the first time in years, perhaps ever; the polyester trousers which were worn for travelling to and from the stinking refineries at which we joined or left the ship were ironed.

People were walking round the alleyways being startled by running into other people whom they thought they'd never seen before and then realising that they were people with whom they'd been working day in, day out for months.

The captain sat in his bridge chair with an expression of mild amusement upon his face. He'd seen it all before. He'd been at sea on the Bank Line ships in the old days down to the South Pacific and then, after that, he'd done a few years on passenger liners on the Australian emigrant trade before jet planes ruined that. He'd been able to control his drinking, which wasn't necessarily common during his generation of seafarers and he'd benefited from the invigorating effects of pumping out all those bodily fluids without suffering the consequences of imbibing lots of poisonous ones. He sucked on his pipe and just made the occasional comment on the arrangements.

The disco arrived on a bum boat and the "guests" arrived shortly after on another. While a studious-looking Filipino from ashore organised the technical side of things, the guests shimmied around, making great play of how amazed they were to be on a ship for the "first time". The Filipino crew proudly showed them around.

The radio officer was over-friendly with a suspiciously young-looking girl. "She only playing," said the bosun to me. "She want him."

"In England we say 'playing hard to get', I said.

"She easy to get. Just take time," said the bosun. "She want to see if she can get handsome boy like third engineer."

"I am not handsome enough for her?" I said

as if I were offended, but being careful to smile when he turned to look into my face.

"She too young," he said, seriously.

"Only joking," I told him.

A woman in her twenties soon grabbed me around the waist while food was brought out. I knew the crew were sitting on three suckling pigs that they'd been brought by the company for Christmas and New Year in a very uncharacteristic burst of generosity on the part of the tight-fisted accountants back at Geordie-Central. I wondered if they were going to be brought out early, on this special occasion. Nope. They were not.

I looked up to see the captain peering over the bridge deck rail. He had that look which either signalled bafflement or amusement; it was always difficult to tell.

"Keep control," he said to me. The mate was in bed and I was the second mate, but I thought this was an undeserved burden. How was I to supervise this. It would soon get out of hand.

"Don't worry," said Osmando, who'd joined the crew of this boat earlier on. "I control things for you." This was good. Even the officers were scared of Osmando and would stop whatever they were doing with one steady look from him.

The party started in earnest. At one stage, I was lying flat on a sill on the poop deck while two silk-clad young Filipina girls sat each end of me, looking up at the stars. This isn't such a bad life, after all, I thought.

A row suddenly broke out. A girl was shouting at the radio officer, who was a bespectacled, very quiet Irishman." She was furious. Our Filipinos were moving in to surround them. I went over. "What happened?" I said.

"We will handle this," said the quiet bosun.

"Eh, yeah, but as the senior white officer," I said.

"You're not senior," said the Geordie chief engineer.

"O.K.," I said."

"You're not senior," he repeated, sounding furious. Actually, this is an old one. Originally, engineers weren't signed on as officers, though chief engineers were, I admit. This was a constant source of aggravation. Eventually, it was decided to shut the engineers up by making them officers.

Generally, though, in the event that the captain was incapacitated, command passed down to the mate. If he were incapacitated, the second mate and so on. The deck officers were governed by law; the engineers generally weren't. Additionally, the engineers were generally dirty and dressed in lube-oil stained boiler suits and didn't look like officers.

Anyway, I conceded authority to the chief engineer. "O.K.," I said, "you solve the problem." He took offence at this invitation.

"I'm not doing your job for you," he said. I sighed.

"What happened?" I asked the bosun who was listening to a stream of Tagalog from the girl.

"She touched the radio officer's genitals and he slapped her," said the bosun. The girl seemed to understand this as she lifted her tantrum to a new level. I didn't blame her for her confusion. I'd thought the radio officer had wanted her.

"I don't want to stay, anyway," said the radio officer. He slunk off, and the bosun thrust a can of beer into the girl's hand and led her away and the incident was over. I turned round, relieved, to find the chief engineer still glaring at me. I threw my arms out as if to say, what's the problem.

He turned round and went over to his boys.

The party went on. One startling incident stopped it in its tracks, though it soon got going again. A Filipina girl came round one side of the companionway, wearing only panties, large breasts bouncing around, with a giggling deck cadet chasing her, and then disappeared round into the other companionway. "Someone should intervene," said the second engineer, but no one did and then everyone turned his attention back to whichever girl he'd been entertaining.

I sauntered up to the bridge. The third mate was there by now. He was looking the worse for wear. "The mate says I'm drunk," he said.

"But he still left you on watch," I replied.

"He said he wasn't staying up here for the likes of me." Actually, it didn't, so far as the real world, matter too much. We weren't likely to catch fire and you can't do collision avoidance if you're at anchor. But, of course, the authorities would have him if there were an incident.

"The chief engineer threw a wobbly," I said.

"He's mental," said the third mate. "They're all mental. Do you think we'll be the same one day?" I shrugged.

"Don't know," I replied. "Maybe. There's not much of an alternative course of action if you're stuck on a ship. You're brainy. You could study. Get some stupid MBA or something and go into a shipping office."

"You hate university because you didn't go," he said, accusingly. The third mate had a degree so was a bit sensitive on this subject.

"Maybe I didn't go because I hate university," I said. "They're so superior, these students. Anyway, mustn't rant. I think the bum boat's going to take those who want to go home away. Is there anyone in your cabin who wants to go home?"

"Nah," he said. "I only had short time."

"And they say romance is dead," I said.

I went round the alleyways, hammering on the doors and shouting that the boat was leaving so all aboard who wanted to go." There was a scurrying and half-naked Filipina girls clutching strappy shoes hurriedly exited cabins. Like the pied piper I led them all up to the poop deck, looked over the side, saw the boat was waiting at the accommodation ladder and escorted them off. Suspicious financial transactions seemed to be going on between some of the older women and the Filipino crew, but I didn't investigate. I didn't want to know what was happening. The three monkeys: see no evil, hear no evil, speak no evil.

I watched as the girls and the DJ clambered down the ladder. They seemed to be quite practiced at this sort of thing. They come back tomorrow with DJ to take off the amplifier etc.," said the bosun.

"And the other girls," I said, hopefully.

"Ah, you know some staying," he said. "You very clever."

"Not so much," I replied. "It's bleeding obvious."

The next morning, the bumboats were back. A few sleepy-eyed girls emerged from cabins, the D.J. and the crew carried the amplifiers and speakers down the gangway and sad goodbyes were said.

We set sail for another port in the Philippines. Once we'd been going a while, I heard a feminine -sounding giggle coming from the deck officer's alleyway. I walked down it until I heard it again and could identify exactly which cabin it came from: it was the deck cadet's. I tapped on his door. He opened it, wearing only a towel.

"And?" I asked him. He faked a look of confusion, then quickly gave up on the charade.

"I didn't realise we were sailing so early," he said. "Anyway, we're still going to be in the same country, so what's the problem?" Hmmm, I thought, the youth of today.

"Well," I said, "she's not on the crew list even as a supernumerary, she's not insured, the captain will be crucified if the office finds out, you will be fired and sent home. No other company will take you on apart from maybe some Thames barge operator or some harbour dredger skipper." He suddenly looked a bit more worried.

"You don't have to tell," he said. I thought about this.

"I know you young kids. If you get found out, you will say the second mate knew so you thought it was all right."

"I won't," he swore.

Hmmm. I thought about this. I was obliged to tell the captain. Yet if I did, the whole boat would hate me and judge me as the Bernie Smalls of the merchant navy. I decided to keep quiet.

A day later, we arrived at the next port. The deck cadet sent the girl down into the boat in which the agent had arrived, along with the bosun, who did some negotiating for him and handed out the requisite payments. I looked on from the guard rail at the top of the accommodation ladder. Problem solved, I thought, and the cadet had solved it himself without the captain having to get involved, which showed good initiative. I suddenly had the feeling someone was watching and looked up at the bridge wing and there was the captain, observing everything. He didn't seem too worried. The cadet, the agent and the bosun had sorted it out and the girl was soon gone and then the incident had never happened. He wouldn't get a rollicking from the Chief Geordie back in Geordie-Central and the deck cadet had a great story for when he got back to Glasgow nautical college. I'd been stupid to have been seen watching the resolution, but never mind.

An illicit affair

Lovelorn cadets were a constant problem. I was on a ship in a Latin American port, and the deck cadet came down with his umpteenth dose. The captain was rolling his eyes and sending in medical reports to the company. Things weren't quite at the modern stage, at which accusations of incompetent management fly out to ships' captains from the offices of executives who've never even been to sea, let alone held a command, but we were on our way to that. The office could mount a dual attack like a Sopwith Camel pilot with his twin machine guns: the captain wasn't looking after the health of his crew and he was costing the company with all these medical expenses. The mate was summoned, given a reprimand for not seeming able to control even one seventeen-year-old boy, and sent down from the captain's cabin with a red face.

The cadet was duly shouted at, old-school style. I'd like to be able to say that, unlike the modern, sit him down, stroke his hair, put your arm round him and work through an improvement check-list with him style, this worked. But it didn't

We were up the road later on and the chief officer suddenly realised that the deck cadet was nowhere to be seen. The boy had only been allowed to come ashore again because he'd given the mate his word he wouldn't go with anymore prostitutes.

The mate stomped around the little banana port, bracing fleapit hotel receptionists until he found him. He, apparently, kicked the hotel room door in, which was stupid as it brought the police into things which took even more money to keep quiet than it would have cost in doctor's fees to fix the boy's next dose had he been left in peace to catch one.

The boy was just about to perform his duty when he was grabbed by the neck and flung off the woman. He curled up in a corner, having banged his head on the wall, and started to bleed, while the girl screamed and the hotel receptionist whacked the mate with the flat of his hand and shouted, "Estupido, estupido." The cadet later told us that he tried to explain to the mate that he hadn't thought the woman he'd picked up was a prostitute and thus hadn't deliberately flouted his authority, an unlikely story.

All in all, a total disaster. I'm sure the captain wished he'd just kept his mouth shut. As a British politician, Willie Whitelaw, once said, "Sometimes, when you absolutely must do something, the best thing is to do nothing."

Something that surprised me, though, was that the rest of the officers looked down on the deck cadet as their moral inferior, not for having sex with a prostitute, which they regarded as perfectly normal and did all the time themselves even though most of them were married with children, but because he'd abused the chief officer's leniency.

The deck cadet, in the face of a shunning which would have done credit to a community of fanatical Amish people, finally had to perform a public grovelling and beg Papal forgiveness. The mate turned his head away in the manner of a wife to whom a husband who has been caught out having an affair with a much younger woman is trying to apologise, and then placed a hand on the boy's shoulder in a sign of absolution. The other officers broke into smiles of smug satisfaction, in particular, irritatingly, the most notorious whoremongers. We were one big, happy family again.

Sometimes, the experienced officers wound up in emotional entanglements. It takes surprisingly little time in isolation, working on one's own in the engine-room on a tanker or staring out to sea on a tanker's bridge before the mind starts to go. Judgement is the first thing to fly out of the window. They were always falling in love with hookers and strippers, even the ones with wives at home.

Tampico and Havana

I was over working on the big ships for a while and decided to look for something different. I soon had a call offering employment on a little ship running between Tampico in Mexico and Havana. This sounded exotic. Cuba was just going through its 'special period' subsequent to the collapse of the Soviet Union during which Fidel and Raoul Castro had to admit that communism without subsidies wasn't sustainable and that the country would have to open up a little. The hotels which had been taken over from the American Mafia and allowed to slide into near ruin had been worked on and improved a little, which wasn't easy to do given the American blockade; and the Spanish had been enticed into the country out of which they'd been unceremoniously booted in 1898, to help run them.

I actually joined in Rio Haina in the Dominican Republic, to which the ship had been diverted for some reason. I joined at anchor, my bags having gone missing on the flight. This missing bag event seemed to be almost procedural. A long line had formed at the missing baggage counter at Santo Domingo airport and I received my bags four days later, anything of value having been removed.

Anyway, the agent took away my passport. This little British company which had managed to get the contract with the Cuban Government had a habit of sending out its seamen and officers without the appropriate visas and trusting the agent to sort it out when they arrived. I, being white and British, merely had my passport taken away by the agent so he could obtain the necessary stamps. Three Cape

Verde seamen whom the company had sent out a month or so previously had been imprisoned upon arrival. The company wasn't bothered and didn't see why the seamen complained; they were still getting paid, weren't they?

I was run out to the ship in a little boat and clambered up the ladder to be met by a huge Ghanaian, who was the second engineer. Actually, I was to find out that officially he was the chief engineer, but the old-school British captain wasn't having a coloured officer over a white man and had insisted on treating the second engineer, who was from Manchester and a buddy of his, as the chief engineer even to the point of switching their cabins around. I found both the captain and his buddy drinking whisky in the captain's cabin.

The captain was ex-Blue Funnel and still thought he was sailing around in the days of the Empire. He was sitting in his captain's chair in full uniform. The grumpy "chief engineer" was listening to him rant on. I introduced myself, and the captain looked down his nose at me and directed me to find my cabin. This trip wasn't going to be fun.

The crew were a Cape Verdean mechanic and two Cuban deckhands. The Cubans had been brought in to replace the previously imprisoned crew who, upon the ship's arrival in Tampico, had gone to complain to the Mexican police about their treatment by the captain and the company and had been promptly accused of mutiny, jailed in Mexico and then flown out.

One of the Cubans was a huge black guy. The captain hated him. I'd never really come across a true, old-school racist. It got quite embarrassing sometimes when the captain went off on one of his rants. This Cuban didn't understand English and didn't seem to take all the shouting seriously anyway but his white companion got offended on his behalf. The Ghanaian did get upset about his own treatment and wrote to the company to complain of racism, but the captain managed to just laugh this off.

Eventually, we went into Havana. I was working flat out, stowing containers. The captain did absolutely nothing. This had been his habit on Blue Funnel years ago and he'd come out of retirement for this little job thinking the world hadn't moved on. I was so tired. He kept telling me that I should see Havana. "Well, who's going to look after the cargo?" I said. "Are you?" He looked horrified and offended at the same time. Once he'd finished shouting, the younger of the Cubans, a fully-qualified chemist apparently, smiled. I just looked at him.

"The old hypocrite," he said.

"He's not a hypocrite," I said. "He's just lazy and out of touch." The Cuban laughed.

"He's a hypocrite," he said. "Do you know where he goes every night? To his black girlfriend's, that's where."

"O.K., he's a hypocrite," I said, and I thought he was a hypocrite not just because he hated black people yet had a black girlfriend, but also because he was always going on about what a great family man he was and how he'd instilled moral principles in his two "fine" sons yet was sleeping around in Havana with a girl a third of his age whom he was, no doubt, exploiting.

We went off to Tampico, in ballast. This was my first time in Mexico. I had no idea what to expect. In Latin America, unless you included Miami, I'd only been to Venezuela for one day and through the Panama Canal without stopping in Panama.

The pilot came on board in red polo shirt and Ray Bans looking like an extremely cool drugs kingpin. The captain took ages to berth the boat, which had the Cubans laughing at him, and then the Mexican stevedores were at work. They seemed very efficient, so I took a chance to slope off ashore with the Cubans. I wanted to look around, but they went straight into the nearest brothel and so I accompanied them. They didn't want to spend any money, though. They came from a sexual paradise and would be back there soon; here they were happy just to drink beer with the girls. I slipped away from them after a little while and went back to the ship.

I had counted on the captain to be paying little attention to what went on outside his office, but, unfortunately, he'd decided to take a very rare walk around. Upon being loaded, a beam had fallen over in the hold and landed on a pile of bags of something and spilt them open, and he was jumping up and down with rage. He saw me and started jabbing away at my chest. I let him calm down and just went on with the work, and he eventually disappeared back into his office. I didn't think he'd fire me; the company would do their usual thing of throwing the responsibility back upon him, doing anything they could to avoid paying any more airfares. In any case, he'd already fired some mates, and had others demand a transfer; it wouldn't do for him to complain to the office about staff again.

Once we'd finished loading, the Cubans reappeared with a tonne of electronics and food which they were taking back to Havana, and we left.

We hit bad weather, which drove the captain to new heights of fury, his office, which was all laid-out neatly, Blue-Funnel style, being turned into a tip. He came up to the bridge, screaming at me. "What do you want to do?" I asked him. "Just run with it? We'll never get there." It was his fault anyway. He could have decided to just stay in Tampico, but he obviously hadn't bothered to check the weather or had been told the forecast by the agent and not listened to him.

I was beginning to work out what his problem was. He hadn't wanted to come back to sea, especially not to a bums and stiffs outfit like this. He'd been seduced by the usual illusion, common to captains of his era from the more self-important companies like Blue Funnel and P & O, into believing that he was someone in society. Consequently, in such situations, there follows the wife who imagines that she, by association, is someone in society, and the too-expensive house and the private school fees, all of which eat into the retirement fund. He bitterly resented that he was on this tub, dealing with a chief officer and mate who wore greasy orange boiler suits, without a personal steward, and being shown no deference by any shore officials. Sometimes, I felt a little sorry for him. And, anyway, he represented, in his own little way, the decline of Britain as a world power, which I found sad.

There was a huge argument. The Cuban government didn't want to renew its charter, which I suspected was because the Cuban crew had complained to their crew agent that the captain was a racist who persecuted them. I knew he didn't like them, which he made no attempt to hide. This came on top of the Ghanaian's complaints to the owners, but this company didn't find it easy to recruit captains with unlimited tickets, which is what was needed while this ship was so far from the U.K. that Home Trade tickets wouldn't suffice, so they wouldn't do anything. The argument didn't come over this directly, though.

We needed to get back to our stomping grounds around the U.K. and Europe. Little ships didn't carry containers that far; we would have to carry a bulk cargo (it was unthinkable to go empty). The problem was all our hatch seals had deteriorated and were now leaking. Any grain would be ruined. The captain intimated that the company had quietly suggested that they should just send the boat over in this condition and put in a cargo claim when, to everyone's "amazement" the ship opened its hatches in the U.K. to find a sodden lump of grain. The captain made a point of being very moral and refusing to do this. However; the company then sent over its thuggish superintendent to intimidate everyone into sorting something out. He wanted me and the new Cape Verde sailors to sit on the side of the hatch, under the tented hatch covers, hammer out the old seals and insert the new ones. The hatch cover hydraulics were in very poor condition and leaked hydraulic oil al over the deck at the best of times. Even if they'd been in perfect condition, the job would still have been too dangerous. The only safe way of doing it was to lift the hatches off with a crane and do it in a shipyard.

The superintendent threatened me with all sorts of violence while the "tough as nails" old-school captain scurried away. I still refused. I thought the superintendent wouldn't want to get into any violent situation while he was in Cuba. In the U.K., it might have been a different matter. He wasn't even staying in a hotel, which was a condition under his visa, so he wouldn't want to attract even a little attention from the authorities, much less be involved in ambulances being called and the rest.

I was fired. Good. A new mate would be flown out but they wanted me off before he arrived so that I couldn't contaminate him. This is standard operating procedure when someone refuses to do something illegal or exceptionally dangerous just because the company wants to save money.

A flight ticket was organised and I was taken off to immigration. This was in an old building on the waterfront which hadn't been worked on since Batista's day along with the other municipal buildings in Havana. Two immigration agents sat smoking cigarettes beneath the no-smoking sign, asked me for a carton of cigarettes, which I didn't have, then reluctantly signed some papers.

"Now you are free," said the agent.

Havana airport was like a tropical bar with a runway attached. I believe it's been updated since. At the time, I don't think it'd changed much since the days when the Cuban middle-class went scurrying across the tarmac to their waiting Pan Am DC-3's, keen to get out while Fidel was still willing to let them go.

I downed a rum and coke, bought a Che Guevara tee-shirt and resolved to question crewing agents more carefully before I jumped on a plane from the U.K. in future.

Shanghai Bound

I joined a medium-sized bulk carrier which was fitted with cranes which meant it would spend time in smaller, less efficient ports than normal. This company had had some of them handed over along with tankers by its parent company. The plan was to employ Filipino junior officers on them, but the company hadn't got round to organising that yet. I had yet again run into that same problem I'd been experiencing in which I couldn't get onto the more enjoyable ships, or couldn't stay on them, at any rate.

Companies wanted to employ third-world (or what was then third-world) officers on the basis that they were cheaper, but they were still often keener to employ Filipino officers on bulk carriers than on tankers, and I still wondered what the official justification was. Did they think that British officers were smarter and so wanted them on the ships on which a catastrophe could lead to them being sued for a billion dollars. Did their insurance companies force them into it with punitive rates if they didn't. I still thought it was a little bit racist. Surely, if you're going to employ mixed nationalities then you shouldn't, morally, keep one race on complicated ships and one race on simple ships, in some kind of apartheid-like segregation. This time, being a little bit more senior than on the previous occasions I'd encountered this, I wrote to the company's offices and asked what was the justification. They said that they did this for financial reasons. I immediately said that when the time came to take the British officers off the bulk carriers, I'd be happy to stay on for

Filipino wages. The office didn't reply to me, but the captain told me that they'd been forced to admit that they didn't want me sailing on them as a junior officer once they'd brought the Filipinos over and, thus, I'd effectively pointed out that their official policy was racist, and they were offended and embarrassed at the same time.

I had my own, cynical, suspicions as to a secondary reason why some companies didn't want British officers on bulk carriers. Subsequent to the sinking of the Derbyshire (a large bulk carrier), with its full British crew, the enquiries had gone on forever. If a ship sank with Filipino crew, it might, though even this was unlikely, get one small paragraph in the British newspapers and that would be it.

Anyway, we were tied up at Longview on the Columbia River and loading the raped hillsides of Washington State onto our ship: thousands of logs. It was quite fun not to be loading stinking oil or dusty coal. The logs were piled up in the hatches; the hatches were closed, and then more logs were piled up on the deck. Once you'd finished piling up the logs on the deck, you dragged big chains up from the sides of the boat and then pulled a zig-zag wire through loops at the end of the chains. The whole edifice was held in place with five or six massive slip hooks. In the event that the ship was likely to founder, the mate's job was to walk along the seven-metre-high pile of logs with a sledge hammer and knock the pins out of the slip hooks, sending the logs over the side. He had little platforms on which he could stand when he did this. Some Filipino deckhand had actually merely been unfastening a chain once in preparation for discharge (on this occasion, there had been other lashings holding the logs in place) and the loop had caught his leg and the chain had flung him into the water as if from a catapult as it leapt free.

In order to move around on top of the logs, you used spiked over-shoes. It was really quite safe.

The American stevedores were a revelation. I was used to dealing with the rufty-tufty Texans; these semi-Californian West Coasters were a whining gang of complainers. If they saw a tiny patch of oil on deck, they immediately started shouting and demanded someone from the crew rushed over and wiped it up for them, not considering that they might simply step over it or pick up a rag and wipe it up themselves if they were that worried about it.

It came near to sailing time and the deckhands set about building a walkway from the bridge, over the logs, to the pilot ladder, hammering in posts and stringing hand ropes through them. "What are they doing?" I asked the mate.

"The pilot won't walk over the logs without it," he said.

"But with the spiky over-shoes it's safer than walking on a poorly-maintained pavement," I said. He shrugged. I was surprised. This place was the end of a two- thousand-mile wagon train route. These people's ancestors had braved wild, native Americans, rattlesnakes and freezing passes through the Rockies and their descendants were a namby-pamby gang of moaners and whingers.

We left Longview and set off down the river. I looked up at the denuded hillsides as we went. I'd been a witness to environmental destruction in my earliest days on tankers when the mates would dump the slop tank overboard, but this was so much more visual. The annoying thing is that some of these Asian countries ban logging in their own territory and yet are happy to consume logs torn from other countries. So hypocritical and selfish. A bit like Australia constantly shutting down coal-fired power stations in its own territory on environmental grounds, yet being quite happy to live off the taxes on coal exports to countries which were cheerfully burning it in power stations which were much more polluting than Australia's own.

The pilot got off. I watched him walking out over the logs, holding hands with a Filipino on each side of him. What a big girl's blouse.

Then we were off to Shanghai. This was going to be interesting. At this time, China had listened to Deng Xiaoping's "Get rich quick" incitement to capitalism speech, but didn't yet know whether it was a serious policy or a trick.

The passage went all right. The captain was a very frightening man, genuinely terrifying. He could have been a highly successful gang boss, had he been criminally minded. He was inclined to stare at you with his cold blue eyes while his massive bulk loomed over you and ask you up front questions about what you were doing with a tone which implied he suspected you of criminal negligence. I would always stammer when I replied, which just seemed to make him convinced that I was a weakling and cause him to despise me even more than I suspected he already did. I avoided him.

We had a cadet on board and this captain despised him, too, just because he was a cadet. He actually seemed to regard him as a lower life form. The cadet was sent to live on a deck below the Filipinos', which was for now non-existent crew whom belt-tightening had got rid of years ago. He wasn't allowed to join us for dinner and had to eat on his own half an hour earlier. God help him if he wasn't out of the officer's mess when the captain walked in for his own dinner. The Filipino cook, a rare nasty piece of work among such genuinely loveable people, used to torture the cadet by taking forever to prepare his meal and then giving it to him only five minutes before the captain was due. The cadet would scoff it and bolt for the door, still chewing. This sort of thing wouldn't be allowed in today's namby-pamby merchant navy in which some surveyor will sit and hold some moaning crew member's hand on an inspection, gently wiping tears from the poor boy's eyes with a scented handkerchief.

I made one amusing discovery. I had been on stinking tankers and bulk carriers and never seen any air freshener on board. Understandable. It was hardly an expense which could be justified to the board. This ship was the sweetest-smelling ship I'd ever been on, thanks to the ten thousand, freshly cut logs. Yet, I opened a cupboard one day and found it stacked floor to ceiling with boxes of pine air-freshener. Maybe a fired captain had put a last, uncancellable order into the ship's agent as a parting gesture to the company, or it could just have been a cock-up.

We anchored outside Shanghai and a battle began between the captain and the company. The company wanted him to sail up the Yellow River with only half a metre's clearance under his keel. The company guidelines stated that a minimum clearance of one metre must be maintained. "Send me a telex, if you want me to do it," insisted the captain. The company wouldn't. They wanted to be able to blame the captain if something went wrong; but the captain was no fool, was strong-minded and didn't give a damn if they fired him as he was fifty-nine and wanted to retire anyway. The battle went on and on. More and more senior figures from the company rang him on the satellite phone and attempted to cajole him, hanging up in a rage when he still insisted that they sent him a telex. Finally, the company gave in. We were to go a little way up the river, tie up between some buoys, and then barges would come alongside, and the logs would be dumped on them for the trip up the river.

The captain had a little, triumphant, satisfied laugh. The mate looked at him with further admiration. The engineers (the usual mix of flinty-eyed, suspicious, bitter, bully-boy Scots and cheerful, friendly, kind-hearted Scots) even conceded that the captain and therefore the deck side had actually done something right for once.

It didn't take long for us to move into position. There was a minor diplomatic incident when the pilot hawked onto the bridge floor and the captain screamed at him and for a moment appeared

71

to be ready to rip his throat out, but the pilot still got his bottle of whisky once we'd tied up.

I stood on the bridge wing with the mate. "Look at that," he said. There was a factory chimney across the way billowing smoke which changed colour as the pollutants which it emitted changed. "And they're just getting going," he continued. "Think what it'll be like once one and a half billion people are polluting away."

In the afternoon, the barges started to turn up. China was still very poor and the workers looked destitute in their smocks. Their foreman literally booted them up the arse as he sent them up the rope ladders. Ten minutes after they were on board, I watched the deck cadet chasing one of them round the bow. "What's going on?" I said to him, once the man being chased had slipped away from him.

"He touched my arse," said the cadet, breathlessly.

"That's sexual harassment," I told him. "You should sue."

All providers of services had to be tipped with Marlboro. The mate sent the cadet to tip the garbage boatmen and gave him a carton of three hundred cigarettes. "Give them two," he said. Soon, there was a lot of screaming and shouting. We found the cadet looking over the side at the departing garbage boat, with a furious expression on his face.

"What's going on?" asked the mate.

"They wanted more cigarettes," said the cadet. "I wouldn't give them any more." The mate looked at the gesturing boatmen, disappearing into the distance.

"They weren't happy with two packets?" he said, mystified.

"Oh," said the cadet. "I thought you meant two cigarettes.

"You should transfer to the office," said the mate, drily.

We were given passes to go up the road. We went up to see the captain to get some money. He wouldn't give us any. "Not after five O'clock," he said. I looked up at his clock. It was one-minute past five. I thought of pointing out that we couldn't come up earlier because we were working, but he wasn't the sort of man to listen to pleadings.

"I have plenty of money," said the cadet, once we were outside his cabin.

We'd been given tickets to exchange for a boat ride to the quay and a taxi ride and so went on our way, trusting that we would find a bureaux de change. We did find one, but then it turned out that the cadet's stack of notes (he was from an upper-middle-class family) were Scottish pounds and the bureaux de change wouldn't accept them. All we could exchange were the few U.S. dollars and British pounds which I had.

This wasn't a total disaster as, at that time, there was only one business in which you might want to spend money in Shanghai and that was a lone Kentucky Fried Chicken. The girls seemed terrified of us. A policeman outside looked as if he might have a heart attack when I suggested that he might let me take his picture, and his hands, waved spastically.

Actually, we did find somewhere else we might have spent some cash, but all our cash had gone by then. This was the Friendship Store. The Chinese hadn't yet cottoned on to the idea that tourists are there to be fleeced, and things such as silk shirts were on sale for as little as the equivalent of four pounds.

We caught a taxi back to the quay, through the grey city and the surprisingly few inhabitants, straining away on their bicycles. I thought of all those bright-eyed, English hippy and dour, Scottish, hard-men teachers whose enthusiasm for communism I experienced during my nineteen-seventies comprehensive school, British education. What a bunch of clowns, I thought. Cuba was one thing: at least the inhabitants had sun, sea, sex and sand; this was just oppression. "Join a union as soon as you can. I can't believe you're suggesting that just because a man built a corporation, he is a fit person to run it, William," etc. etc. Yeah, yeah. Change the record.

We had one more, little thing to do before we set sail for Vancouver. We had to send one of the Scots home. "Give us a photo for the documents, captain," said the senior immigration official. After a few phone calls to the engine room and a bit of searching, the captain looked up at the immigration officers.

"We don't have a photo of him," he told them.

"That's all right," said the senior official. "Just give us a photo of any one of you. You all look the same to us."

What happened to the others?

I started to investigate what my colleagues from my training days at Warsash were doing. One had gone to South America, married a local girl, shacked up in a beach house and then got bored with that and gone to university to become a marine lawyer. I was amazed by both his choices. He was the most unromantic person I'd ever met; I'd never have thought he'd be the type to try to settle down in South America. And he was the least studious person in our class at Warsash. How he'd worked his way through all that mind-numbing case history to become a marine lawyer, I had no idea. He's a multi-millionaire now.

Another had dropped out of a promising cruise ship career to become an unsuccessful artist.

A third had despaired of coming home from long trips, jumping into his second-hand, cheapest-on-the-market Porsche and pulling up outside 7/11's on sink estates and dazzling the check-out girls, and had given up his seagoing career to become an insurance agent.

A few were working on ferries, which used to be all right before a monopolistic company bought up or drove out of business all the smaller, happier, family run, ferry companies.

One guy had been made redundant eight times as company after company switched to cheaper third-world officers. This was a difficult situation for the Government. Companies didn't want subsidies to continue with the employment of British officers anyway (they just wanted to get rid of them) but should the Government use the law to protect British seafarers' employment as the Americans did? The Americans just ended up with an uncompetitive merchant navy full of overpaid American officers which wouldn't last five minutes if it had to compete in an open market. There wasn't the will in the U.K. to protect British seafarers' jobs anyway: the memory still lingered of disastrous seaman's strikes; the firebrand behind a few of them had been a man who was now a prominent Labour minister, but he was safe and secure in his ministerial Jaguar and didn't have to face the consequences of the bitterness he had generated.

All in all, I was doing all right, hanging in there, surviving. I didn't have the stomach to go into the persecution industry which was what the governmental regulation side of seafaring was all about; I didn't have any business ability and I didn't want to work in an office. I loved trains, but I didn't want to spend forty years in packed, slam-door commuter trains as my father had done.

Up the Amazon

I went back on the bigger ships. I had a fascinating voyage up the Amazon. It took days to get to our destination and things went even more slowly when we got there. I went up the road with the stocky, Geordie engineer and insisted on taking the usual Filipino bodyguard. The Geordie moaned that he could take care of himself. "I know you can, but I'm no fighter," I said, "and I need someone to take care of me." I'd only had two fights. One opponent had thrown a punch at me, missed and was carried headfirst down a concrete staircase by the momentum, and the other had been so astonished that a placid guy like me had hit him back that he froze whereupon I tried to do as much damage as I could before I was pulled off him.

We ended up in some rickety bar built out over the river. A few girls in spandex immediately started throwing glances our way, and the Geordie lunged out of his chair in their direction. I grabbed his shirt collar and hauled him back down, which wrenched my shoulder. "Careful," I told him. "Their boyfriends could be around." He dismissed this with scorn, but, all the same, he took a look around and. seeing some very big guys eyeing us from the bar, slid back into his seat. My Filipino bodyguard fingered his knife. I hadn't realised he'd brought it and I glanced down at it with trepidation. "Best not to stab anyone except in an emergency," I said. He made a face as if to say he would reluctantly comply with my stipulations. I knew he was probably hoping that something would happen which would require retaliation.

A girl whose breasts were subjecting Spandex to a stress test which I felt would exceed anything the manufacturers had envisaged rose from their table and slid into a seat at ours. She placed her hand on the Geordie's knee. There followed some sing-song, Brazilian Portuguese and then she said in English, "I love your blue eyes." The Geordie beamed, vindicated. Her friends came over and one heavyweight sat on my lap while her lighter companion sat on the skinny Filipino's and put her arm around him and stared into his little, black, killer eyes. He looked up at her and I assumed as she hadn't squealed that he'd slid his knife back into its hiding place before she'd sat on him and thus avoided causing her to accidentally stab herself in the bottom.

Slowly, the Geordie and his girl began to get intimate while I shot nervous glances at the local boys at the bar. Suddenly, his girl jumped up and said, "Do you want to come to my place?" The Geordie's eyes lit up. He couldn't believe his luck.

"Yeah," he said. The girl smiled.

"O.K., I'll just ask my boyfriend," she told him. To our horror, she marched up to the boys at the bar and said something to the biggest. He looked over to us, seemed to be considering the matter, and then nodded and spoke some rapid Portuguese to her out of the side of his mouth. She smiled and came over to us and cheerily announced that she had permission. "But," she said, "you have to pay me and no anal sex." Our jaws fell open.

Finally, the Geordie recovered himself and said, "~Well, let's go then." He stood up and was gone. and I was left with the other two girls and my Filipino bodyguard.

"I wonder if we'll see him again," I said.

"He will be all right," replied the Filipino. We were soon in some shacks by the river ourselves. It ended up being the usual third-world, entire-family-invited party, with bottles of some local firewater, for which I paid, passed around, and piles of roast chicken, for which I also paid, appearing in front of us.

We got back to the ship to find that the Geordie hadn't returned and the worried captain was fuming. We would be sailing soon, with or without him.

He soon turned up, happy as Larry, indulging in a massive kissing bout on the quay before he wearily climbed the gangway. "Idiot," said the radio officer, looking at him from the manifold.

"Why?" I asked him, mystified.

"H.I.V.," he said.

"H.I.V.'s a myth, I said. I saw a documentary.

"You're both idiots," he said and then he disappeared into the accommodation.

We went to the Dutch Antilles and this was more than just another refinery. Some of us ended up in some kind of an official brothel. I wasn't sure whether it was owned by the Dutch Government or the refinery or was just approved by the authorities. We sat in worn-out easy chairs, smoking cigars and being entertained in the little hut type places which the girls rented and then filled with electronics. Prostitutes all around the world had some kind of obsession with electronics from what I had seen.

We had a British bosun who organised the Filipinos, this ship having only recently changed over to Filipino crew and the company wanting to maintain some British control over them for a while. He was a grizzled, old story-teller, who would have been labelled a raconteur if he'd been wearing a velvet jacket and sitting, similarly sozzled, in some London club with a gang of solicitors and stockbrokers instead of in a Dutch brothel with a group of merchant seamen and Columbian prostitutes. He found it difficult to leave with us when it came to sailing time and some of us had to gently heave him to his feet and steer him out of the door; a heavy-breasted topless Columbian girl in panties not making the job any easier, clinging to him and begging him to stay longer.

Once we'd left port, his optimistic, enthusiastic personality soon took over from his gloom which had been brought on by the abrupt end of festivities. "Colon," he said to me, breathlessly.

"What about Colon?" I asked him. He smiled.

"Just follow me," he said.

We anchored off Colon, which is at the entrance to the Panama Canal and the terminus of the trans-isthmus railway. In years gone by, when filled with Americans, both servicemen and chancers on the make, Colon had been full with garish nightclubs with slinky Rita Hayworth-style singers. Now it was decrepit and dangerous. It's just awaiting redevelopment, actually, and in the same way that the old town in Panama City has turned, since Noriega's enforced departure, from being a no-go area into a swish, safe, nightlife area, will soon be redeveled; but, at the time, it'd more or less been abandoned by the Panamanian authorities.

We went up the road, the bosun and I, with our usual gang of Filipino bodyguards, who were, incidentally, well-armed with knives and knuckle dusters. The bosun seemed to know where we were going. "Donkey show," he hissed.

We went down some stairs beneath what had clearly once been an elegant hotel and passed some huge black bouncers and were in a nineteen-fifties-style nightclub complete with red carpet and red, flocked walls and a dimly lit stage. The bosun ordered a round of drinks which were brought over by a slinky cocktail waitress, and an emcee took to the stage and said something in Spanish into the old-fashioned microphone which stood in the middle. Then he proceeded to shift the microphone to one side and drifted into the wings. I took a look around the room. There were a few Panamanian business men, a couple of paunchy, elderly Americans in Hawaiian shirts and a younger American in a suit with a woman who looked as if she might be his wife.

A middle-aged, Hispanic woman dragged a naked Indian or native-American-looking girl out onto the stage and then, once she'd walked off, a huge black guy wearing only a loin cloth marched out and grabbed the girl by the throat. Then he whipped off his loin cloth, bent her over, and had his evil way with her. The Filipinos were whooping and the Hawaiian-shirt-wearing Americans were red-faced and panting. I worried that one of them was going to have a heart attack. I looked over to the other side of the room at the yuppie American couple. The woman was staring fixedly at the scene. Her husband was grasping her hand so tightly that his knuckles were white.

The male performer exhaled and the girl grunted and they stood up and faced the audience and smiled upon receiving enthusiastic applause from the Filipinos and tepid applause from the Americans.

"This isn't what we came to see," said the bosun. By this he didn't mean that it was offensive, just that it was a nuisance and unnecessarily delaying the donkey show.

The young Indian girl and the huge black guy were soon swept off the stage, anyway, and the emcee announced the star performer, a scruffy donkey, which was led on, swishing its tail at imaginary flies. A frightening-looking, middle-aged woman followed him on. "I hope that's not his co-star," whispered the bosun in the disappointed tones of someone who'd turned up at the Dury Lane only to find the understudy had replaced his favourite actress. Fortunately for the morale of our little party, she was just the technician. She ran a lot of O-rings onto the donkey's member and then beckoned to the wings, and a young, very pretty girl danced on, smiling at the audience as she did. The donkey proceeded to make love to the girl, unable, though, to achieve full penetration due to the O-rings. After a minute, the older woman invited the audience to chuck money onstage upon receipt of sufficient of which she promised to peel off the first O-ring, allowing the donkey to penetrate deeper. Our

Filipinos embarrassed us by flinging dollars at her. Normally, Filipinos are a little bit careful with their money, but all restraint was forgotten. The bosun sat smiling as there was so much money going the woman's way that he wouldn't be required to make a donation. This performance was repeated over and over again until there were no more O-rings left on the donkey's member. The young girl turned to face us and gave a bow and I wasn't absolutely sure, but it seemed that the donkey dipped its head in acknowledgement of the audience's thunderous applause. I turned to look at the bosun. "Promised you a donkey show and I delivered," he said.

"I thought you meant some kind of gymkhana thing," I protested.

"Good one," he said.

We sat on through a few more performances which all seemed a bit 'Saturday night at the local working mens' club' after that. Then we scuttled out into the streets and along to the boat pick-up point. "Are we safe?" I asked the bosun, looking around, as we went through the deserted streets.

"I don't think so," said the bosun. "We don't have any guns, or, at least, I don't think we do." We made it though.

The captain was a bit judgemental and I suspected from his behaviour in the morning that he wanted to have it out with me over my joining the crew on this little venture, but he didn't say anything. He probably thought it wasn't worth the bother.

Studying for a higher certificate

I had been promised over and over again by companies that they would send me back to maritime school to study for my unlimited chief officer's licence. None ever did. They would just find some excuse not to and then, if you complained, would let you resign and hire some other mug who believed them.

There was the option of paying all the costs myself. I started to look around. Warsash, where I had been a cadet, was in a very expensive location and it wasn't a lot of fun anyway. It was in a village with three pubs, one of which had patrons with a tendency to wrack grievous bodily harm upon maritime students who went in, something which the police and judiciary treated lightly, both, obviously, being on the side of the locals. There was a very snooty yacht club whose members seemed to be a bit insecure about these sixteen-year-old cadets who were already more highly-qualified and more experienced seamen than them wandering in with the odd local girl.

There was Glasgow, but I'd once met a boy who'd attended that school and had just been walking down the road outside and accidentally had eye contact with a local who'd immediately taken offence and slashed his face with a Stanley knife, so I wasn't up for going there.

Apart from a few minor places, that left South Shields. All the Geordies on the ships seemed to think fondly of it. It was in the middle of some E.U. economic disaster or something area, so the fees were subsidised. Rent was very cheap. I sent in my application forms.

Soon, I was living on the road on the hill outside the college and studying hard. The college's attitude was very different from that at Warsash. Warsash had been more theoretical; the lecturers at South Shields were constantly putting you mentally in the position of being the captain faced with difficult decisions.

I was getting an additional education: into how the other half lived. I'd never really spent much time in the North and the surprise at what went on was huge. The few Southerners in our class didn't know whether to be amused or sad; sometimes, we were both at the same time.

The whole area had been run down by the economic disaster of the collapse of British industry. The shipyards which had turned out a thousand ships were just about gone, only a few boutique organisations being left. The mining was over. There weren't any factories. And the whole of the precarious society which remained was kept going to a minimum standard only with government subsistence.

The social costs of this were huge. The men sat around, uncertain what to do. The social security kept the families going, not the fathers' non-existent salaries, so the society was totally matriarchal; the men just drifted around, staying with one woman for a while and being a sort of semi-father to her kids, some of which might be his, and then moved on to another woman. Although it's sacrilege these days to say that boys need a father figure, they didn't seem to be doing well without them. Without fathers, some went straight off the rails.

The police had given up on crime and just confined themselves to their police stations with the exception of a trip out in the riot van to the front of the nightclubs on a Saturday night when recalcitrant clubbers who hadn't been sorted out by the bouncers were bundled into the back and dealt with while onlookers eat their kebabs and commented with amusement on the gentle rocking of the vans with each unseen thump or kick received by their victims.

The Bombay Indians, who made up a huge proportion of the senior classes at the college did very well with the local girls. They were polite, shared the enthusiasm for brand name sports gear, weren't tight with money, didn't get drunk. The other successful contingent on the romantic front were the Iranians, whom the local girls insisted on referring to as Persians.

It was striking, sometimes, to see some of the local girls, whose fathers had obviously been sailors. You'd turn round in a pub and there would be a truly exotic-looking girl, perhaps with Arabic features and mocha skin, ordering her Bacardi Breezer in a Geordie accent. Some of these girls could, and should, have been fashion models, but I found that there was little understanding of the opportunities to be found in London and this was such a matriarchal society that the inhabitants of the town were all afraid to leave their "mams".

One beautiful girl said to me, "I don't have the chance to go to London and sit around waiting for something to happen, anyway. I don't have the money."

"Listen," I said to her, "just get off the train, go to the City and sit in some bar which the stockbrokers go to and you'll have a boyfriend on a hundred thousand a year before the lunchtime session is over." She didn't believe me, or wouldn't listen.

One day, I took the little tram-style train through Jarrow etc. to Newcastle. Some of these places were even more run down than South Shields. I wondered if the Government could have done more. If you think about a shipyard and the myriad professions it supports and the difference between jobs and careers in that and the alternative careers the government suggests such as tidying up in Sainsbury's, you might think it was worth subsidising the shipyard to keep it going. But then again, in the face of unionism and intransigence on the part of some of the workers, is that going to succeed.

The course went O.K. I failed a few things but just retook them. The Marine and Coastguard Agency didn't help by constantly updating things, but, then, they were being bossed around by the International Maritime Organisation, an interminable committee and branch of the United Nations. In addition to the irritating little periodic exams which had been introduced to take the strain off students by not subjecting them to stressful big exams, we still had the stressful big exams, just in case. I failed one of these and had to retake it. The first three questions were calculations and I knew I'd got them right and thus had over sixty per cent of the marks and was so exhausted I didn't answer the last two questions. Apparently, there was some obscure rule which I didn't know about according to which the candidate had to attempt all questions. Great. Another three hundred pounds in the government's kitty. At least, with a bit of luck, it'd send some of it to South Shields to help single mothers with their food bills.

I failed the orals, too, but on what I'd call ideological grounds. At the end of it, the examiner said, "I'm sorry to tell you, you have failed."

"Why?" I asked.

"Well, on the going aground scenario, you didn't mention the SOPEP (anti-pollution policy).

"Yes," I said, "but I ran through all the actions to save the ship and the crew etc."

"Yes," he replied, "but we've been told by the Blair government that we should fail candidates who don't show enough concern for the environment." Blimey, I thought, there's the government plastering Iraq with uranium-tipped missiles and I'm being penalised for not showing enough concern for the environment in my little exam scenario in some Northern town the Chianti-swigging lefties in London gave up on years ago. Never mind. I took it again, showed tremendous, heartfelt concern for the environment, and passed.

There was a lot of sadness that the year was over. Some people had treated the place like a brothel, some people had just sat in pubs and enjoyed living in a social environment. Despite all their economic handicaps, the local population seemed to enjoy life and their enthusiasm had been infectious. Only one local girl departed camp with her Southern boyfriend. This girl had once been out with us and told us that she'd only ever been to Newcastle, which was twenty minutes away, once. She'd never been over the Tyne on the ferry to North Shields. And she was nineteen, I don't know how she got on, apart from years later, someone told me he thought they'd got married and had a couple of kids.

Suicide is painless

I went onto some more big ships and found myself, once I'd boarded one of them, surrounded by the fallout from a tragedy. There'd been a suicide, a not uncommon occurrence on merchant ships. There was often little sign of the emotional turmoil building up to these events and no one who would have cared if there had been. I remember one ship on which I'd sailed on which a very young third officer had disappeared over the side. He was newly married, but caught an uncurable social disease from a prostitute in Santos on his first trip after the honeymoon. He was actually totally in love with his wife and hadn't been able to face the ordeal of telling her of his affliction. Of course, feminists will probably say his actions merited punishment and, possibly, his suicide, but it was still quite sad.

The suicide on this new ship hadn't been so neat and tidy. The second engineer, having received the customary Dear John letter, had hung himself in the duct keel, which is a long tunnel which runs along the centre of the vessel beneath the hatches on bulk carriers, through which all the electrical cables and pipes are routed.

The body had been discovered by a sixteen-year-old engineer cadet who'd been sent down the duct keel by the third engineer, to check on something. Due to an electrical fault, the lighting in the duct keel hadn't been working, and the cadet was finding his way with a torch which, as with most torches on ships, in my experience, had a nearly spent battery and soon dimmed and then went out. He was nearer to the bow end of the tunnel, at which there was a ladder leading to a hatch on deck, than to the engine room and so continued along the duct keel, feeling his way until eventually he bumped into something soft, suspended from the ceiling. Running his hands up and down it, he suddenly realised it was a body. Panicking, he stumbled his way to the ladder, climbed up to the hatch and emerged into the sunlight, bruised and bleeding as a consequence of bashing into fittings as he blundered along. The A,B.'s working on deck looked on in amazement as he stood there, screaming in panic, terrified.

The chief and third engineers retrieved the body, bringing it down the duct keel to the engine room on the little trolley which ran on rails along the passage. The captain was waiting at the exit and the chief engineer passed him the camera and he took some more photographs. I was on navigational duties on the bridge and didn't see anything, not that I would have wanted to. Entries were made in the log. The meat was thrown out of one of the freezers and the body placed inside. Actually, we weren't sure for how long we'd have to carry it around. It often happened that the first port of arrival for a merchant ship with a corpse on board would refuse to allow the corpse to be discharged, and sometimes the second and third and so on. Macabre, but there you are. Shore authorities often don't want the hassle of dealing with something like that.

So, the ship settled down. The engineer cadet came round. He was still a little bit twitchy but he seemed all right. Some of the crew were moaning about the meat having to be thrown out so that the second engineer's body could be stored, but there was no way that the captain could have allowed the cook to continue to use the same freezer for storing meat for consumption.

Once the corpse was gone and the freezer had been loaded with fresh meat, no doubt to the annoyance of the shipping company's budget-minded superintendent, things seemed totally back to normal.

Unbeknown to everyone else, though, the third and chief engineer still had some fun to be worked out of the situation. Without bringing the new second engineer, who was a really nice guy, in on it, they had a little plan. The third engineer, with a supportive pat on the back, sent the engineer cadet up the duct keep again to do a job at the far end. He waited until he reckoned the cadet would be much nearer to the far end than to the engine room end and switched off the breaker on the newly-fixed duct-keel lighting circuit. The engineer cadet, presumably experiencing flashbacks, blundered along and collided with another pair of swinging legs. Screaming, he emerged once again through the forward entrance onto the deck, to even greater bewilderment among the A.B.s, who didn't seem to be able to get through an afternoon of chipping paint without such an incident.

It turned out that the third and chief engineers had strung up the dummy used for drills. Their laughter soon turned to consternation, though, as the engineer cadet had a total psychotic breakdown and had to be sent home from the next port, still gibbering. Of course, the captain got the blame officially, but, unofficially, the chief engineer received a severe reprimand from the superintendent. The third engineer used the Nuremberg defence that he'd simply been following orders, which has worked every time apart from that onetime at Nuremberg when it didn't.

Abandoned in Argentina

I went to Argentina and spent two weeks waiting for a ship which never arrived. I journeyed daily from the hotel to the offices of the shipping company's agents and sat down on the hard wooden chair opposite the impossibly beautiful secretary while I listened to the ceiling fan revolving and the blare from the horns of the dockside traffic through the open window until the agent himself, wearing his sports jacket and sporting his pencil moustache, deigned to appear from his inner office and loftily inform me that there was no news.

I was in a tricky situation. I'd got on the plane without a contract. This used to be quite normal. Sometimes your contract would never arrive, and, so long as you got your salary on time every month, you wouldn't worry about it. Technically, I wasn't an employee. The company could just discard me. They didn't even have to pay the hotel bill, I think. This was a ropey old company I was joining, something which I'd known. If I complained to the employment agency which had put me onto the job, they wouldn't have any sympathy. They would just tell me I was stupid to have got on the plane without a contract in my hand. Of course, had I rung them earlier and said I didn't want to fly out without my contract, they would have said I was being paranoid, because they would have been worried about their fee.

Daily, I returned to the hotel. It didn't seem as if a call was going to come suddenly, so I started to explore Buenos Aires. I'd always heard that it was the Paris of South America. In some strange way, I thought it was even more like Paris than Paris. The architecture was the same.

All the people were, of course, of Italian descent. The women were gorgeous; the men looked like Italian racing drivers. They were quite friendly, too, although the women were not friendly at all in a romantic way. I wished I'd got here earlier, before the Falklands War. Apparently, then you could milk being British for all it was worth, which was quite a lot in Argentina. Now, it was best to keep quiet about being British, and all because our Government reinforced the Falklands after they'd been invaded rather than before, which, I believe, would have been a superior military strategy.

I found, eventually, a girl who wanted to show me around. I'd been sitting on the main drag, which, incredibly, was more or less empty at midnight and yet full to over-flowing with crowds at two in the morning. This seemed to be the last bastion of nineteen-twenties elegance. Girls who looked about thirteen sat in long black dresses, smoking outside fin de siècle cafes. Miraculously finding a little space, a few couples tangoed. Whether this was a demonstration or a spontaneous event, I had no idea.

This girl sat down next to me. I immediately decided that she was some kind of rebel. She had spiky hair instead of some elaborate coif. She was still smoking, though: it would have been rebellious not to smoke in Argentina. I puffed away on my cigar. "Tourista?" she said.

"Seaman," I replied.

"Marinero," she said.

"Si," I said, affirming this.

"American," she said. I blushed.

"British," I told her. Her face bore no expression. I wondered if she were going to get up and leave. Then the waitress came over and the girl gave her her order, so it looked as if she weren't.

"My father is British," she said. "Well, he was born in Argentina. He went to a British school."

"He went to school in Britain?"

"A British school in Buenos Aires," she replied. She waved her hand around as if to indicate the whole street. "You like all this?" she asked me. I shrugged.

"What's not to like?" I said. "I'm waiting for a ship, but I'm beginning to wonder if it will ever arrive."

"Are you getting paid?" she asked me. Good point. I hadn't thought about this. I should be. I should have been from the moment I left my home.

"I hope so," I told her.

"I would like you to see Buenos Aires, properly," she said, "so you don't think we Argentinians are evil." I laughed.

"I don't think Argentinians are evil," I said. "What makes you think I do?" She shrugged.

"The war," she said. I laughed again. "Don't laugh," she said.

"It's just that I think the Falkands War..." I saw her face flush, "Guerra de las Malvinas," I said, hastily, "was about elections and fishing rights and oil etc."

"Good," she said. She sipped her coffee and waved the waitress over. "Pay and let's go," she demanded. She was definitely a little mad. I found out later on that all Argentinian women are considered a little mad. Apparently, the city of Buenos Aires has more psychiatrists per capita than any other city in the world, all of them, seemingly, ineffectual.

She took me into a darkened tango club and sat me down in a red velvet chair at a tiny round table on the edge of the dance floor to watch the display while she went over to chat to a skinny, intellectual-looking man in wire-rimmed glasses who was evidently a friend. I looked on as the dancers did their thing and thought of the contrast between this performance and the donkey show at the similarly-decorated venue in Panama.

The girl came over to my side. She suddenly

seemed to be relaxed and vivacious. I enjoyed chatting to her quietly while the Astor Piazzola music played on the gramophone which was presumably being used instead of a modern sound system in order to supply more atmosphere.

After a while, I got up and went to the toilet. On my way in, her friend grabbed my shirt sleeve. "Be careful of her," he whispered. "She is crazy." He swirled his finger around while it was pointed at his head in that now-offensive gesture which is used to indicate that someone has mental problems. I wondered what to say; he seemed to be expecting a reply.

"Thanks for the tip," I said, finally. He nodded with satisfaction and turned his attention back to the performance.

Time went on. I couldn't obtain any information from anyone about this ship and I began to wonder if it even existed. I made some calls from public telephones to the U.K. The employment agency still said this was none of its business. The agent still stonewalled me.

The girl showed me around town some more. Once, we went into a basement bar and I heard some home-counties accents over in a corner. Five minutes later and some bearded Englishman in shorts and sandals was standing at my side. "And you are from where?" he said.

"Sussex," I told him. He tilted his head back and looked down his nose at me, his rheumy eyes appearing to be unfocussed.

"No, you are not," he said. I laughed. He was confused by the South Londony accent.

"Crawley," I added.

"Ah," he said. "I understand."

We ended up over at their table, drinking wine. The barman had gripped my sleeve and whispered, "Communistas," as we went.

The Englishman's girlfriend was a stern, grey-haired Argentinian lady who lectured me on the benefits of communism.

"I've been to Cuba," I said, and she launched into a paean of praise to the glorious Fidel. I was waiting for a pause to tell her that Cuba, which had been the third-richest country in Latin America, was pretty poor after forty or fifty years of communism, but no pause came. Finally, her husband bluntly interrupted, which shut her up.

"Che Guevara used to drink here," he said.

"Do you know that Cuban joke about him?" I asked. The communists looked at me blankly. "Well," I continued, "after the revolution, they were all having a committee meeting and Fidel asked if anyone was an economist. Che Guevara put up his hand, so Fidel made him Finance Minister. After the meeting, Che asked Fidel, "Why did you make me finance minister?" Fidel said, "Because you said you were an economist." "Oh," said Che, "I thought you said is anyone a communist." The background to the joke is that Che Guevara was such a useless finance minister that he destroyed the Cuban economy so quickly that even Fidel was embarrassed. They all frowned. This communism was a deadly serious business and not a fit subject for jokes, said their looks. They were so hostile that I laughed. The girl dragged me back to the bar.

She took me to Boca, which was a former slum which'd undergone some sort of weird gentrification in which the houses had all been painted bright colours. I was having a good time, but this couldn't go on forever.

She launched into some mad story about losing her virginity in Mar Del Plata and then having a massive fight with her boyfriend and walking out on her family and then going back. It just went on and on. Then she said that she'd been unfaithful to me the previous night. "I don't want to hurt you," she told me. "I shouldn't have told you." I looked at her, wondering if she were joking. Then I had to decide how to react. Laughter wouldn't be right; jealousy would require acting skills beyond my meagre talent in that department. I decided to just look hurt. I lowered my eyes and kicked at a tuft of weed in the pavement.

"I'll cope," I said, sadly. She held a hand to my jaw and tiled my face in her direction. I fought the urge to burst out in laughter and then turned my head away and went on walking in the direction of the bus stop with her at my side.

Upon our return to my hotel, the day manager started to complain to me about my bill. "Isn't the agency paying it?" I asked him. Turned out the agency'd been sent an invoice for the time up to the end of the month but hadn't paid it yet. I shrugged. Were they going to throw me out. No point worrying about it. I certainly wasn't about to pay the bill myself. If they tried to insist, I'd just tell them I wouldn't and see what the Mission to Seaman and the British Consulate had to say.

We went up to the room, some rapid Spanish passing on the staircase between the manager and the girl, and I sat and looked out through the dirty window at the River Plate. "He says that I am not really allowed up here," she told me.

"What did you tell him?" I asked.

"I demanded to know if he thought I was a prostitute," she said.

"And?"

"And he didn't reply. Maybe I have brothers who will come and kill him if he said something like that about their sister."

"You don't."

"He doesn't know that." Just then, there was a knock on the door. I opened it and a messenger boy stood there with the day manager behind him. The boy gave me an envelope. It contained a flight ticket to London for three days' time. I looked up. The manager had a satisfied smile upon his face, and the boy seemed to have an expectant look upon his. I pulled out some damp peso notes and handed them to the boy and then closed the door.

I turned to face the girl. "I'm going home," I said. She was sitting on the window sill, staring out at the river herself, now.

"Good bye," she said.

Great Britain

I wanted to get some ship-handling experience if possible and went onto smaller vessels around the United Kingdom and near continent. Counter-intuitively, the way to gain ship-handling skills is to be on smaller vessels. What happens with supertankers etc. is that they get within a mile of the berth and they have a pilot on board and they get within half a mile and they have tugs. Technically, the captain is simply receiving guidance from the pilot, but as the pilot is highly skilled, berthing big ships on this river or in this harbour every day, knows the local tides and depths inside out and is often speaking to the tug skippers in his own, foreign, language, the captain is reduced to being an observer, though, of course, he will still be blamed if any incident occurs: that suits everyone: the pilotage authority, the harbour master, the coastguard., the media. Therefore, a supertanker captain can blithely cruise through his entire career from sixteen-year-old deck cadet, to sixty-five-year-old captain doing very little ship-handling. He used to at least do the anchoring, but now, in a lot of places, a pilot even comes on board for that.

The small ship captains are still looked down on, though. Even the Maritime and Coastguard Agency, which is the agency in Britain which currently issues certificates of competency, looks down on them. They might say they don't, but when you go for your unlimited licence oral examinations, you can see a faint expression of disapproval on the examiners' faces when they glance through your discharge book and see the entries for the small ships. Of course, the examiners are successful big ship captains.

Anyway, I soon got a job. The manning agency, which was the old employment pool in Southampton, sorted me out. The boss had laughed when I'd told him what I wanted. I was sent along to a company office and dealt with the usual middle-aged harridan. Don't think I'm prejudiced, though. These women, who took over personnel throughout the shipping industry when the shipping companies decided they didn't want to employ worn-out old captains with a reputation for being nice old boys, have since been replaced by twenty-year-old girls with hand-out university degrees and attitudes, who just cause complications.

The lady smiled at me and handed me a contract. I went home and then didn't hear anything about joining instructions for a while. I rang the office and this time got one of the up and coming young girls with attitude. "You're joining in Hull on the second of the month," she said. "Where exactly in Hull?" I asked her. "I don't know," she said, angrily. "Well, how am I supposed to find the ship if I don't know where to join it?" I asked her. This sent her ballistic.

They gave me a mobile number. Mobiles were just coming in and ship's staff were delighted. Once they became efficient and office staff were constantly on them explaining to skippers exactly how they should run their ships, despite never having worked a day on board any ship in their lives, the enthusiasm would fade.

The captain was a little man with little-man syndrome, a belligerent, aggressive guy who was also extremely intelligent and highly sentimental. I sometimes thought I could just write a book about ships' captains. There was such variety and I never met a boring one. This skipper had a problem hanging onto second officers or they had a problem hanging onto their jobs when around him. I couldn't say he was unfair, but he was unforgiving. He liked tough guys which meant I, who'd routinely been abused by mates over the years for being too soft, was on dodgy ground. The Geordies had just blamed my easy-going personality and lack of aggression on my being a Southerner, but this captain was a Southerner so I wouldn't be let off the hook on that account. He had a chip on his shoulder over his not having a Master Unlimited, or, in fact, even an unlimited watch-keepers certificate. This situation had arisen as he'd been a late starter, walking away from jobs in which I am certain he would have been very successful and which would have eventually led to him starting his own business and becoming a multi-millionaire. He routinely lambasted holders of unlimited certificates as being practically useless. Well, they didn't have his ship-handling skills, of course, but they did manage to get three=hundred-metre vessels full of flammable spirits or gas across the Pacific and the Atlantic.

There was a lot of bullying going on on board. I'd rarely seen that on the bigger ships. The second officer whom I relieved was a very well-spoken, extremely nice public-school boy and was routinely persecuted by the mate, a pot-bellied, little jobsworth. It was with some satisfaction that I was to see the mate get his come-uppance at another's hands later on.

The second engineer was a tough guy and bullied the chief engineer, an exceptionally nice guy who'd come out of retirement, relentlessly, pausing only when he temporarily focussed on another victim. On the bigger ships, I don't think he would have been tolerated. He might have tried it on with the Filipinos, which wouldn't have ended with a happy outcome from his point of view.

The pay on this company was basically at the subsistence level. Secretaries earnt more than even the captain. Well, why shouldn't they earn more? Because they don't need years of experience and they don't risk getting flung in jail for something which wasn't their fault. The others were all trapped, though. Their employment was on a rotation basis: a few weeks onboard, a few weeks at home, and they all had families. Listening to continuous updates on this family life thing was new to me. I'd been on the bigger ships when there weren't mobile phones and the married men just seemed to alternate between total paranoia and indifference when it came to their wives. They often didn't know whether their wives would even still be around when they got home and had no way to find out so their attitudes were understandable. This lot were more like shoreside employees. The only thing which really surprised me was that apart from the two nice guys, the second mate and the chief engineer, they all constantly complained about their wives.

I was finding out about the state of Britain's ports, too. This was a revelation. Being British, I had naturally assumed that Britain's ports were the best in the world. What I found was that some looked as if they'd last had major investment in Charles Dickens' day. I remember Liverpool: the quay was like pumice. If our ships slightly touched the wall, it would crumble away, and an officious little man from the port authorities would be on hand to record the "damage caused by the vessel" in his little notebook. We once went into a drydock in Hull and were waiting patiently for the gates to close and three men came out with a very long lever, dropped the end in its socket and spent thirty minutes walking round and round, winding them shut manually. This could have been due to a machinery failure, but even so, it wasn't a good look.

Some of the shipyards we went in and out of weren't that great, servicewise, either, and the attitude wasn't as good as it might have been. Up North, so much would go missing. Security would have a massive rant at the captain if one of the crew had brought a girl in, screaming about "bringing prostitutes into our shipyard" normally without any evidence at all that the girl in question had been a prostitute, but just turned even more red-faced if the skipper dared to mention that ship's equipment had disappeared and gone out of the gates in the workers' Mark II Capris. "Where's your evidence?" they would demand.

Stuff going missing was mainly a problem for the crew who simply had to try to do the job without that equipment, but, once, I remember that, throughout the yard period, the yard had been so helpful with the crane and then at the end an extortionate bill was laid upon the superintendent, every lift having, apparently, been priced individually. Then of course, the superintendent was embarrassed because he hadn't read the fine print and the company was furious.

It didn't seem to occur to the yard owners or workers that if they simply did a good job for a reasonable price, they'd ensure repeat business. I think that this may have been why the Government tired of throwing cash at these traditional industries.

There were further signs of deterioration in Britain's fabric. Sometimes, we'd wait for our ships in these Northern ports and be put up in hotels with 'Grand' in their titles and you imagine in the breakfast room in the morning, how they must have looked in their Edwardian heydays, when Britain actually had shipowners, and the faded and crumbling décor would have been pristine, and the staff would have been on hand to minister to every little desire; and now you'd be sat there and there would be couple of fitters sitting in their filthy boiler suits, smoking cheap cigarettes and swearing away. I thought it was very sad. I suppose you could regard it as a tribute to socialism that there wasn't that class distinction in some of these towns anymore (everybody was poor) but I didn't see it that way.

The great bonus of working on the coast was, of course, rotation, or so everyone said. But I was starting to see it as kind of having a stop/start button for your life. You'd just get going on something, and it was time to go back. I found that my new found ability to join societies etc. wasn't that much of a benefit: people didn't like it when you just disappeared for three weeks and then came back and tried to carry on as normal. Girls didn't want to wait for you for three weeks, any more than they wanted to wait for you for five months. In fact, I thought it was better just to do your five months on a supertanker and then get off and buy a ticket to Brazil of Thailand or somewhere else like that. This whole 'building up relationships' thing was just a mirage until you were ready to give up sailing and take a job in an office.

Sexists?

There was new experience for virtually all of us: working with a woman. The captain on the opposite shift from that of the little martinet, which I'd now joined, suddenly looked worried. "They're sending us a female engineer," he said. Some of us looked at him in mystification, some, in fury. This was the sort of thing that raised the hackles among traditionalists. Then the captain shrugged and left the messroom.

"It's not fair," said the third engineer. "I can't be a lingerie model." I looked at him while he sat there, unshaven, pot belly bulging through his filthy boiler suit where a button had popped off.

"You could try," I said.

"Haha," he replied.

Once she turned up, all the predictions of chaos among the more anti-crew were quickly proven correct. It transpired that she'd sued her previous company for sexual discrimination. "She's got previous," I said to the captain. "She hasn't got previous," he said. "She was victimised."

Despite being plain and overweight, she glared at anyone who lingered in her path too long wondering which way to shift to make room for her to pass as though he were considering becoming a rapist, beginning with her as his first victim.

I tried to avoid her. I was sitting in the officers' messroom, hurriedly making my way through the tough beef, and she ambushed me. "You're going on holiday to Egypt," she said.

"Yeah, I am," I replied.

"You'll hate it; it's horrible," she said. I tipped the rest of my dinner into the bin and slid out. Later on, the captain said to me. "She's been complaining to me that you're avoiding her."

"Is that an offence?" I asked. He considered this.

"Might be," he said.

Soon, he changed his attitude. I was sitting in the officers' messroom and I heard this sudden screeching from the crew messroom, in which the captain, having originally been an A.B., preferred to hang out. The woman was having a go at him, but I couldn't make out the words. Then he appeared in the officers' messroom door. "If you ever speak to me like that, I'll punch you in the face," he said, jabbing his finger in my direction.

"What did I do?" I asked him.

"I'm just warning you," he said. I shrugged, and then he appeared to realise he was making a bit of an idiot of himself and disappeared. It transpired that our shift would be getting off a day late and she'd torn into him in front of the crew and had actually been quite offensive. Doing a day extra was no big deal, anyway. It was unavoidable, sometimes. Who cared: one less day at home. Sometimes it worked the other way and we got an extra day at home at the expense of the other shift.

Things deteriorated. She started to shout at the deckhands and tell them they weren't doing enough and yet this, though possibly true, was nothing to do with her: she was an engineer and only the fourth engineer at that.

Oddly, the bullying second engineer who entertained himself terrorising the nice-old-boy chief engineer and bouncing the engineer cadet off the bulkheads had decided he liked her. "It's because she never tried it on with him; he's so intimidating," said someone.

The captain was still fuming over her explosive attack on him. We had on board an ex-Grimsby- trawlerman who said to me, "I'll stir it."

The captain was suggestible, and this trawlerman went up to him and said, "Now you must understand, you have to make allowance for women's' problems." That did it. The next time she had a go at the skipper, he said, "I'm not giving you special treatment on the basis of women's' problems." She exploded, her face furious. I hid behind the chart table until she stormed off the bridge. The Grimsby trawlerman had had his fun, but the captain was lucky. For saying something like that in the Me Too era he would have been fired immediately.

I thought of asking for a transfer. "You can't," said the captain. "That's discrimination."

"What, it's discrimination if I say I don't want to work with a woman."

"Of course, it is," he said. I could say I didn't want to work with him, but I liked him and that sort of thing eventually piles up in the company's "Ammunition to be used against the captain when it suits us" file.

She soon solved the problem herself, however. I was on the bridge when the internal phone rang. I picked it up. It was her, sounding unusually trite and speaking so softly I couldn't make out what she was saying.

"What?" I said. "I can't hear you. Try to speak up."

"It turned out that she'd slipped on the engineroom stairs and injured her leg, and she had to be taken off on a stretcher at the next port.

"Broken?" said one of the deckhands with a hopeful tone as the ambulancemen carried her away. The captain turned on him.

"No, not broken," he said, with distaste at the question.

The captain, a really nice guy, but with boundless enthusiasm and a love of "inappropriate humour," was soon being harassed by the jobsworths at the company as to the cause of the accident.

"She's so fat, her leg simply gave way," he said, with a chuckle. He was soon on the receiving end of a reprimand for that.

I wondered how men who were working in offices got on. Were they walking on eggshells?

Around the Continent

I decided it was time to move on and got a job on a small bulk carrier owned by a very old British steamship company. I joined in Cardiff and no sooner had I met the captain than I was wondering what I'd done. He was a Belfast man, strong IRA supporter, up from the ranks type, very aggressive, with a real chip on his shoulder. "Don't think you'll find any soft option on here," etc. etc.

"I wasn't looking for a soft option," I replied, "just a job." I left his office, my head spinning, and went and found the mate. The mate was a Bombay Indian. He was, I found, a favourite of the captain. According to the mate, a lot of people didn't want to sail with this captain, and the mate, himself, didn't want to sail with some of the other captains, anyway, so they were a team.

The deck crew and oiler were Cape Verdes. The chief engineer was British and the second engineer was Indian. The cook was a toothless old hangover from the old British merchant navy deep sea companies. I was the second mate.

I found out that this little boat used to have twenty-three crew in the nineteen-seventies. Now it was getting around, doing the same job, with eleven. The life the old crew must have led, it must have been wonderful. They'd had two stewards to look after them. They had enough staff so that they could organise days off. Th decline of the British merchant navy could be summed up just in the comparison of this ship's manning then and now.

One of the worst effects of reduced manning was that we were dealing with a two-watch ship instead of a three-watch ship. This meant that I and the mate were in a constant state of exhaustion. On some journeys we were supposed to get an extra watchkeeper, but the company would just organise an exemption. So, we were driving around like this, barely able to keep our eyes open. The authorities were aware of this problem and their answer was increased prison time for people who fell asleep on watch. Talk about treating the symptoms rather than the cause. It wasn't as if someone was going to say, "You know what, I won't fall asleep and run into a tanker because I'm going to get six months instead of only three."

"You shouldn't be on here," said the chief engineer to me once we got to Belfast, which was our first destination.

"Why?" I asked him.

"The only jobs going soon will be on tankers and you should be continuing to specialise on tankers." I should have listened to him, but, actually, I began to enjoy myself on this little boat. The advantage of having a total martinet as captain is that things run like clockwork: no one tries anything on. The Indian mate was of a far higher standard than a lot of British mates you would get on a boat this size because a lot of companies around Britain were still a little bit prejudiced and he couldn't get the sort of job which his qualifications and abilities merited. The Cape Verde crew were highly-skilled. I think they inherited the talents of their Portuguese forebears who, while not particularly brilliant at running their empire, undertook some spectacular voyages in building it, braving the unknown. Their race, incidentally, is something of an accidental, genetic experiment: almost all the male DNA comes from white men and almost all the female DNA from black women.

We hit a great number of ports and I got to see some places which I hadn't visited on the bigger ships. We had a contract for ore cargos out of a place called Odda in Norway. This was quite an amazing destination; you went miles and miles along one fjord, turned a bend and went miles and miles up another. Right at the end of the second fjord was this tiny town with a little industrial plant. I thought I'd take a look and checked with the mate and he said, "Yeah, sure, take a wander." No sooner had I got to my cabin and begun peeling off my boiler suit than the captain came barging in. He leaned into me and I thought for a moment that he was going to hit me. "Don't think you're going skiving," he said. His face was bright red.

"I was just going to take a spin round for ten minutes," I said.

"You're not," he told me. "There's work to do." Then he stormed out.

Ten minutes later, he came into my cabin again and said, "It's O.K, you can go, don't be long."

"I went and found the mate in the cargo office. He was looking sullen. "What's up with him?" I said.

"Don't worry," he replied. "Just go and have a look around and then come back." I thought some more about this. I reckoned that the captain had been under the impression that I'd just got up and wanted to go out. Actually, I'd been working continuously for ten hours. Probably after the first time he came barging in, he went and found the mate to complain and the mate explained this to him.

I took my stroll around. The place was beautiful. I could imagine Viking longboats sailing up this fjord and being hauled onto the beach. I went up to the top of the town where there was a beautiful lake and you could see the quarry.

We loaded up and then the pilots came on board again and we fired up the engine. "Don't drop the wires in the water," the mate was yelling at the linesmen. He wanted them to carry them along the quay to the vicinity of our winches and then drop them, but the Norwegians just said, "They're too heavy," and dumped them where they were. The mate mumbled something in Hindi which didn't sound very complimentary. I don't know if he was worried that they'd get caught on the propeller. We weren't variable pitch, so it wouldn't be turning until we moved off.

We went to Copenhagen and where the Norwegians had had three linesmen, the Danes sent down only one. "Are you sure you can carry that wire along the quay?" I asked him, "because three Norwegians couldn't manage it." "Ja, ja," he said and calmly picked up an eye and dragged one along.

Actually, the Scandinavian countries reminded me of Northern England, full of tough-looking skinheads in football shirts and blonde girls. To what extent the similarities between the inhabitants were due to the Viking legacy, I didn't know.

We set off to Algeciras with a cargo of scrap and a new mate, a lugubrious Scotsman. He had been a container ship captain and this was just a little retirement job for him. He was constantly full of doom and gloom. The chief nicknamed him Fraser after the character from Dad's Army. I quite liked working with him, though, At the end of the day, personnel managers just fling people at ships, but cultural homogeneity does, sometimes, make things run more smoothly.

The mate's dire predictions of the effect of the scrap cargo upon the ship were proven correct. Leaks from the ballast tanks sprang through the holes in the plating which the scrap had made and we needed to bring on a repair outfit.

While we waited, the company sent the captain home and sent a new captain out. He was a thoroughly nice guy. Suddenly, it was as if we were on a different ship. It never ceases to amaze me how much of a difference a change of captain can make to the atmosphere on board a boat. I think the mate liked the new captain. He and the old captain had both been alpha males, which never worked out. That was like having two head chimps in a zoo. The new captain was just a polite public-schoolboy who'd taken a few wrong terms and was now on the bones of his arse, working for this company, instead of being a captain on a P and O cruise ship or something. He invited me and the mate into his cabin for a drink and instead of driving home "this is going to be a working ship" etc. principles, he proceeded to launch into raconteur-like ramblings. The mate listened patiently; I encouraged the captain in his story-telling.

Despite the ship having half the staff it'd been built to run with, we suddenly started having a good time. We went off to North Africa and then up and into Hamburg. On the way into Hamburg, the pilot started ranting about immigrants. These weren't even illegal immigrants, but the official invited workers. The captain raised his eyebrows, but, just when I was thinking he was a kind-hearted lefty, we were out on the bridge wing looking at a massive fire which lit up the night sky and he turned to me with a smile on his face and said, "Remember Dresden." I shot a nervous look through the bridge wing door, worried that the pilot might have heard, though the pilot was still ranting, even more loudly, actually, in the hope that we'd be sure to hear him outside, and he wasn't paying any attention to us.

I wanted to continue with this company, even though the pay was terrible, but as with a lot of "British" companies at the time, it was taking advantage of the loose employment law relating to seamen to just empty officers on an ad hoc basis. Sometimes you would get an offer of another trip, sometimes you wouldn't. You could wait and wait and nothing might happen.

A visit to Bellevue hospital

I decided to try very hard again to get back onto tankers. No luck. They wanted people with a solid, tanker-only record and senior officer experience on tankers, as I'd been warned. I thought I'd try looking around in the U.S.A. I had C1/D1 visas, but these were for people arriving on, joining or leaving commercial ships. In those days getting a visitor's visa was pretty easy, though. You just went to Thomas Cook, bought a flight ticket, handed over your passport, signed something, gave them an extra five pound and it was yours. There was no stack of paper, fingerprinting and interview to prove you weren't some imaginary, Islamic terrorist.

I flew to New York on Kuwait Airlines, amused to find that the plane had only a handful of passengers. This was before the airlines were so efficient at filling planes and when some countries didn't care if their airlines made a profit so long as they were around to fly their flags.

Immigration was a doddle and I got on the subway and wound up in a YMCA which was combined with a youth hostel. I took a shared room in the youth hostel bit, finding my companion was a young British guy on his way home from a failed attempt to immigrate to Toronto.

I took a look around New York the first day. I'd been to the refinery berths in New Jersey, but that'd been on some worn-out old tanker with a mate who didn't believe in giving junior officers anytime off, so I'd only seen Manhattan in the movies. I was impressed with the positivity and the energy which was missing in the U.K. although its absence in the

U.K. was disguised by the mini-boom caused by the flood of North Sea Oil money into the economy. Since then, with the Great Recession having blasted the United States economy into pieces, that positivity and energy has moved on to Asia of course, but at this time, apart from in Japan, Asia was still fighting its way out of the third world.

I thought on the second day I'd start poking around in some shipping company offices. Even a lot of American companies flagged their ships overseas so the lack of United States certificates and immigration papers wouldn't be a problem. I didn't get the chance, though.

I got caught up in the New York violence which I'd always imagined was exaggerated for the movies. In the middle of the night, there was a hammering on our door and my room companion leant over from the top bunk and opened it. Its travel was limited by the security chain which he'd put on in what I thought had been a fit of paranoia. Blearily, I asked him who it was. "Just some guy who can't find his room," he said. The alarm bells should have started ringing, but, for some reason, they didn't.

I decided that I needed to go to the toilet and got out of bed. Stupidly, I didn't think about things. I was still wearing my money belt as I didn't trust my room companion. However, because there was no air-conditioning and it was so hot in the room due to the New York summer, I'd taken my tee-shirt off. I walked straight out into the corridor and along to the communal toilets like that.

As I passed the lifts, a young, muscular black guy eyed me. I didn't think anything of it. Then, as I was turning away from the urinals, he walked into the toilets and I was just aware of a flash of movement before he hit me. I collapsed to my knees and then tried to rise to me feet and he hit me on the head again. He was so professional he just said, "Give me the money;" he didn't use any more violence than he thought he needed. I opened the money belt and handed over the American travellers checks and British driver's licence which were the sole contents. I looked up at him while he studied the licence. He looked concerned. I thought maybe the New York authorities investigated more when victims were foreigners. Sadly, later on, I was to find out that the reverse was the case.

When I think about this incident, I wonder if the media isn't a little hard on the American police who shoot to kill rather than waiting around to see what happens. If I'd had a gun and training and been willing to shoot during this incident, I'd have had a split second to decide whether I was going to. Of course, turns out my attacker hadn't been planning on killing me, but I didn't know that and neither do the American police who get caught up in these things. Of course, they get into trouble for "profiling", but they have experience of dealing with poor, violent, young black men that the media doesn't. Even in that split-second they might think they see signs in their adversaries facial expression that they've seen in the facial expressions of ghetto kids who've tried to kill them when they've been in similar situations. Maybe they think, better to sit through months of interminable enquiries than risk having their wives and kids weeping at their gravesides.

I rose to my feet and staggered to the lifts and went down to the lobby. Once the lift doors opened, I felt woozy and had to lean on the wall; then I started towards the desk. The nightman looked around from his bank of keys with a tired expression upon his face. A look of horror came over him. I stopped in my tracks. Did I look that bad. Then I looked down at the floor beneath my feet. There was a little pool of blood and, when I looked behind me, I could see that a trail of it ran all the way into the lift.

He didn't move though, and I continued on to his desk and leant on it. Then he just reached out, silently, and picked up the phone and dialed the police and the ambulance service.

I think I fainted. The next thing I knew a young policeman was leaning into me and saying, "We're taking you to Bellevue."

"That's the lunatic asylum," I said, bleary-eyed.

"It's the free hospital," he told me. His mate smiled at me. Some ambulance workers hoisted me up, their arms under my shoulders and steered me through the doors and to their vehicle.

They all took me into the waiting room at Bellevue. "Listen," said one of the policemen. "We've got to get on with our shift." I shrugged.

"Thanks for coming to the hospital, anyway," I said. The speaker gave me an amused look.

"You're taking this kind of well," he said. I shrugged again.

"I'm from Britain."

"This sort of thing happens a lot in Britain?"

"Eh, no," I replied. "but, anyway..." Then they were gone.

I sat there for hours. It was total mayhem. There were other police bringing hard-eyed, young black men in wearing handcuffs, girls who looked about twelve hugging their mothers, with blood running down their inner thighs. The medical staff flew around, never once pausing in their administrations.

Eventually, a nurse grabbed me and took me in to see a doctor. He was an upper-class Brahmin. I could tell this from the polite way he spoke to me and the fact that even though he was dealing with emergency after emergency he didn't have a hair out of place.

He sprayed my face with some anaesthetising chemical and then started to sew me up. "Welcome to New York City," he said.

"This place is like something out of the Vietnam war," I told him. "The hospital, I mean," I added, for clarification.

"I missed out on Vietnam," he replied. "But it probably is."

"What you doing working in the National Health?" I asked him. "I thought all American doctors wanted to make the big cash." I was going to say, were money-grabbing bastards, but caught myself just in time.

"That's only in the movies," he said. "I'm already rich. My family's rich."

"Ask not what your country can do for you etc." He smiled. "I suppose I'm lucky I wasn't killed," I told him.

"This happened inside or outside?"

"Inside," I replied.

"Well," he said, "this is a bit bad for inside, but, yeah, outside you're lucky if they don't kill you. It's almost impossible to get a conviction in New York without the victim as a witness."

"I suppose a woman might have been raped," I suggested.

"Hey, in this town they rape men," he told me. I looked at him. "I'm not joking," he said.

Suddenly, the patrolmen appeared in the surgery. "Hey," they said, "we finished our shift and came back to see how you were doing."

"That's very kind of you," I told them. "I think I'm going to be O.K." They shook my hand and went out and then came back a few minutes later and handed me a cup of coffee and a newspaper.

"Listen," they told me, "we brought you a newspaper so that you can see that there are people worse off than you in New York." I smiled and thanked them, and they chatted to me for a while, telling me that tourists usually mentioned Hill Street Blues and asked them if they'd ever shot anymore (they hadn't) and then they were gone.

"Nice guys," I said to the doctor."

He finished sewing me up and bid me adieu.

I was just walking out of the main doors and a very young, black nurse grabbed me. "Where're you going?" she said. "You can't go out into the street like that." She took me back inside and over to a wash basin and cleaned my face, and then I was outside again.

I though that the first thing I'd better do is get my American Express travellers checks replaced. While I was sanding in the queue, the American matron behind me started pouring out sympathy. "Poor boy," she said, solicitously "Where are you from?"

"Britain," I told her.

"Listen," she said, "You should visit Florida where I'm from. It's much safer down there. Don't judge the United States by New York." Then she stuck her hand into her purse and pulled out a fistful of dollars. "Do you need some money?" she asked me. I was staggered.

"Eh, I think I'm going to get my travellers' cheques replaced so I don't need it," I said. "But thank you, anyway."

"Don't judge the United States by New York City," she repeated.

The clerk took one look at my swollen and stitched face and didn't bother asking any questions. He just scribbled something onto his pad and handed over replacement cheques.

This wasn't the end of it, though. I went back to the YMCA, and the desk clerk told me I had to have an interview with their security officer. I looked around me and then the clerk pointed at a little glass-partitioned office, and I went over and stuck my head in the door. A guy who looked like the sheriff from some movie set in the Deep-South looked up at me, quickly worked out who I was and bid me sit down.

"This is only the fourth incident in the thirty years I've been here," he said.

"When were the other three?"

"In the last year."

"Someone comes in, books a room, mugs someone in the middle of the night and then checks out in the morning," I told him. He snorted. He didn't like me playing detective. "What were the other descriptions?" I asked him. "Mine is one hundred and fifty pounds, black."

"Nothing like that," he replied.

"Well, what were they, then?" He made a face and flipped open a file.

"One hundred and fifty pounds, black. Listen," he said, angrily, "this theory is just your opinion." I rose from the seat. "Where are you going?" he said with irritation.

"You're not going to do anything, so what's the point in my staying?" I replied. His face turned red and he flipped a business card over to me with something hand-written on it.

"You have to go to this precinct," he said.

At the precinct, I was taken in to see some fat detective who was sitting on the side of his desk, belly hanging over his waistband, massive gun on his belt. He looked at me with total disinterest when the desk clerk announced me, and then took me into an interview room. I looked around me. I was surprised by the whole ambience. I had always thought American cop shows were exaggerating when they depicted their police stations as being bare and poor-looking. They weren't.

The detective was very aggressive. "You're going home," he said, accusingly.

"Pretty soon," I told him.

"So, what's the point in us investigating? You won't be around for any possible court case." I shrugged.

"If you find him then maybe you can persuade him to give up his life of crime and you'll save some other people from being mugged," I told him. From his look, I thought he was going to hit me. He threw a mug book in front of me.

"Take a look at that," he said. "See if you recognise anyone." I flipped through it. There were hundreds of photographs of identical-looking, young black men.

"They all look the same to me," I said. Then I realised this was a mistake. He had the moral upper-hand now. He could paint me as a racist if there were any complaint that he hadn't investigated. He just slumped back and looked at me. "I suppose I should go," I said. He slung his business card over to me.

"If you think of anything else, you can ring me," he said.

Despite this, until I boarded my flight, every other American with whom I had dealings was solicitous of my well-being and dripping with sympathy.

Once I got onto the British Airways flight, though, I was home. Despite my swollen face, none of the stewardesses asked what had happened to me; the British couple whom I sat next to for nine hours didn't think to ask.

Americans, with the exceptions of the YMCA security officer and that detective, were, I thought, a lot kinder than British people, something which never gets mentioned in Britain, obviously.

The City of New York sent me a form to apply for compensation, but I thought of the patrolmen coming back to the hospital on their own time to see how I was doing and then bringing me a cup of coffee and a newspaper, and of the Florida matron and her offer of a fistful of dollars, and I I didn't fill it in. Anyway, I'd been punched in the face and sewn up. People get punched in the face and sewn up on merchant ships all the time and it's just normal. There's never any suggestion that someone should receive compensation.

Last Fling

I wanted to get back onto tankers. I spoke to some of my friends. "You want to get on Shell?" they said.

"I do," I replied. Shell was the last decent tanker company which employed British junior officers.

"You can't," they said. "You've got to be a company man. You're not. You don't care about all that company ethos. You're not going to go wandering around, telling everyone who'll listen what a wonderful company Shell is. Even if you got the Shell symbol tattooed on your arse, their personnel department isn't going to believe you."

They were right. Shell didn't write back to me once I'd sent them my c.v.

There was one company which still had a reputation for being nice to its employees and which employed British junior officers: a car-carrier company. I wrote to them and waited for a reply while I went to work temporarily on some ferries. Britain's major ferry company wanted me to work for them on a regular basis. I would have to give them a commitment. "So," I said to their captain on the ferry on which I was working at the time, "you're going to give me a permanent contract?" He looked irritated.

"They're not taking people on permanently, anymore, not on this ship anyway."

"So," I said, "you want a commitment from me that I'll take on temporary contract after temporary contract, but you won't offer me any benefits or guarantees yourself?" He looked even more irritated.

"So, you don't want our permanent job?" he

said

"Not on temporary contracts," I replied. "Why should I offer you a guarantee when you don't offer me one." He looked offended.

You might think employing people on endless temporary contracts was illegal, but shipping companies can do whatever they want; your employment is with some P.O. box in Bermuda or somewhere similar and employment law only covers you to a bare minimum.

The car carrier company came through, anyway.

I went on board and found the captain. He disliked me, instantly, but I wasn't bothered. The boat was spotless, which I was later to find was due to the demands of the car companies. The cabins were all pine and the showers were bigger than those in a lot of apartments. We had our own T.V.s with video players, and recliner chairs. We had electronic charts on the bridge, which I'd never seen before. What we didn't have was a third officer. I was finding that every time I'd been promoted, my old rank had simply been abolished. So, again, I was working on punishing schedules.

We called at all the usual, decrepit Northern British ports, some ports in the Netherlands and then some in Spain. It wasn't a bad life. We had Latin crew which was all right, but the captains and officers still bemoaned the enforced redundancy of the British crews. They hadn't been sufficiently outraged to quit themselves, in support, though. The company had been around a while and for over twenty years they'd had a great time, sailing around with full British crew and third officers, the commercial guys in the offices finding it difficult to minimise port times and maximise efficiency because the modern communications hadn't yet come in.

There was something alarming for someone such as I, who was still relatively young: there was no promotion. The captains and chief officers were all in their fifties and sixties and knew they would never get another job, and wouldn't ever resign from this company. They fought retirement, too. There were also hints that the company wanted to replace the junior officers with Latins. It seemed to me that there was a worldwide conspiracy to get rid of all British junior officers and I was going to be one of the last victims.

The maritime press had always insisted that Britain needed ex-seafarers to fill all the shoreside jobs which required maritime experience. Well, what was starting to happen was that the authorities and shoreside companies began to fill those vacancies with either foreigners or people who didn't have any maritime experience. Those in charge could always say, "Well, we can't find British seafarers." Well, of course you can't, because you didn't force shipping companies to employ them.

The rot really set in when Britain started to issue Certificates of Competency and Equivalent Certificates of Competency to foreigners and then allowed foreign masters and officers to sail on British ships. British shipping companies don't even need to flag out anymore to fire all their British seafaring staff.

I wondered how long this job would go on.

It was quite fun, though. The ports on the river Scheldt in the winter were so cold your teeth would chatter sometimes, but the pilots were good company. I actually liked the Dutch pilots more than the British ones. The British pilots would rebuff attempts at conversation, which I thought was a little bit selfish. "But I'm stuck on here with only Latin A.B.s for company," I protested. "I hardly ever see the other officers." All to no avail. The Dutch were happy to chat away. After a few months, I was familiar enough with some of them to ask such things as, "Has your daughter got rid of that terrible boyfriend, yet, pilot?"

Then, after Holland, we could trundle down to Spain. The ports we were calling at were mainly in the Basque country. I found the Basques fascinating. It was highly likely that they'd found the Newfoundland fishing grounds centuries before Columbus made his explorations of the Americas. They were rumoured to be the survivors of Atlantis. Their language was unrelated to any other. They had strange skull shapes and blood groups. All the women, for some reason, dyed their hair the exact same chestnut colour.

Our main destination was reached by sailing through a gap in the cliffs, which on a biggish ship was quite something. This was the epicentre of ETA support and the walls of our favourite café were filled with photographs of the martyrs (as the locals referred to them). Once in a while, an ETA member would blow himself up by accident (or so the authorities said) or die in prison, and there would be a strike. The employees working on discharging and loading our ships would gaily carry on, though. Nothing stopped shipping. I remembered all those sanctions breaking gran and gas cargoes carried on ships on which I'd been sailing.

Up in the home ports, though, I began to be alarmed, and, this time, over national economic security and not just my personal job security. We did some amusing things, such as taking left-hand drive cars from the U.K. to the continent and then bringing right-hand drive versions of the exact same models from the continent to the U.K., but I noticed that while we always left the continent full, we frequently left the U.K. half empty and sometimes with only a few second-hand pieces of machinery on board. Could the U.K. balance of payments really be as good as the Government said it was.

This job went on for a few years and then, finally deciding that the management just did not want us Brits and that there would never be any promotion, I quit to study for my Unlimited Master Mariner certificate, and went up to South Shields.

The number of British students seemed to have dwindled even further. I wondered how many more British Master Mariners there were going to be.

I sat through the lectures, which mostly concerned legal issues, things over which the master, in these days of modern communications, had little authority, although he carried all the responsibility and would be the victim of a cynical legal system if anything went wrong, and then it was into the exam room.

I sighed. It was the examiner who'd failed me for my chief officer's orals. I sat down and he went through the usual, aggressive questioning. I sent him back the answers I knew he wanted to hear, which bore little relation to how things happened in reality. He seemed to be looking to fail me, but finally, he sighed and said, "O.K., I suppose you've passed." Wow, I thought. Kids spent three years studying some humanities subject at university for a few hours a week and then were given rolls of paper bound up in scarlet ribbons as if they'd discovered a cure for cancer; merchant seamen spent ten years sailing through storms and studying to get a Master Unlimited certificate and it was, "I suppose you've passed."

I stood up, and suddenly he smiled and shook my hand and said, "Good luck." I'd written thirty-five letters to shipping companies a little while before this and not received any offers. In fact, only two of them had even bothered to reply. I wondered if I should tell him that I was possibly facing enforced early retirement from the sea and looking forward to a potential new career collecting shopping trolleys from outside supermarkets. You had to be careful what you said to these examiners, though. One student, having passed his Master Unlimited, was asked, just after being handed his signed paper, "So, you think you're ready for a command?"

"I think I need a little bit more experience," he'd replied. The examiner promptly took the piece of paper out of his hand and ripped it up.

"Thank you," I said to the examiner and then I turned and left.

It was true, I was struggling to get a new job.

I wasn't that bothered about having left the car carrier company. With no promotion, it was a dead end, and the superintendent was using every trick in the book to get the Brits off, fighting the union tooth and nail. In any case, they were reducing the conditions: two months on, one month off instead of six weeks on, six weeks off.

I really had made things difficult for myself by deviating from tankers. I should have got senior tanker officer experience under my belt. But then, I was still fairly young, who wanted to spend six months poisoning himself on some tanker, perhaps getting his face burned off if he went onto a chemical tanker.

I would just have to look around.

Postscript

This was all twenty or thirty years ago. I often wondered what had happened to the British merchant navy and if there were any remains and then I found them, quite by accident. I keep my licence updated (something which the International Maritime Organisation makes harder every year) and decided to take one of the necessary courses at a little maritime school owned by a British guy and staffed by cheerful Filipinos, in Phuket, Thailand.

I'd thought that the other students would be yachties, but to my surprise I found that they were deep-sea, British tanker captains. They were generally around sixty and working for Chinese owners. They'd been gradually driven out of the shipping fleets owned by the multi-national oil companies. An intermediate step in this process had been when they found themselves working for the customary P.O. box in a tax haven. They said that this was so if their tanker was involved in an accident, then the oil company's shipping division could say, "Nothing to do with us; the captain is an independent contractor". I suspected that this was just cynicism and the oil companies had just been keen to avoid social security payments for them. These captains hadn't found this stage in the transition very satisfactory as the oil companies on the one hand told them they weren't employees anymore, but on the other hand demanded the usual company loyalty.

So, now they were running Chinese ships with all Chinese crews, sailing between Australia and China. They were married to Thai wives and living fairly happily in the more Westernized parts of

Thailand, baffled by their half-Thai children, spending a lot of their time dealing with the immigration authorities and swapping tips on how to satisfy them.

This is what a thousand years of British maritime history had come to. All those shipping lines with their evocative names: Shaw Savill, Pacific Steam Navigation Company, Blue Star had disappeared and with them the vast majority of British seamen. who in their heyday, after the war had numbered two hundred and fifty thousand, and when this last little group of hold-outs retires, then it'll all be gone, for good.

Made in the USA
Middletown, DE
17 January 2020